AMERICAN INDIAN FACTS OF LIFE

A Profile of Today's Population,
Tribes and Reservations

BY GEORGE RUSSELL
SAGINAW CHIPPEWA

NATIVE DATA NETWORK

9027 North Cobre Drive
Phoenix, AZ 85028

Website: *www.nativedata.com*

ISBN: 1-881933-12-1

TABLE OF CONTENTS

Sophisticated Indian civilizations existed long before Columbus accidentally arrived to the New World. There is considerable speculation with regard to the origin and timeline of the arrival of the Indian people to the continent. Scientific discovery and technology indicate that Indian tribal history may be much older than has been generally accepted. Indian people also have their own versions of origin and time.

American Indian population, tribes and reservation demographics are complex and in perpetual transition. Only 22% of the American Indian population live on reservations — which means that 78% live off reservation. Seven out of 10 American Indians do not marry other American Indians. Do the math and project those numbers a couple of generations. The 78% will become disconnected and the 22% will be severely diminished unless there are some dramatic changes with regard to blood quantum requirements for tribal membership.

Almost everyone agrees that American Indians have legitimate grievances that have not been equitably resolved. However, most American Indian issues are politically obscured by current national and international crises.

The only thing for sure in this life is change. Adaptability is short-term evolution that is an absolute for the survival of a species or a civilization. American Indians can no longer rely on the benevolence of the United States government for the necessities of life. They must take control of their destiny by education, political solidarity and economic independence.

The research of your "family tree" as a document for future generations is up to you. There are several necessary steps to begin your genealogy research.

The Study Guide has four parts with a total of 38 questions. The format is fill-in the blanks with follow-up essay questions that may be answered on a separate sheet. When you can answer most of the questions, you will have a basic understanding of American Indians.

You'll Be a Man, My Son
Rudyard Kipling

If you can keep your head when all about you
Are losing theirs and blaming it on you,
If you can trust yourself when all men doubt
    you,
But make allowance for their doubting, too;

If you can wait and not be tired by waiting,
Or being lied about, don't deal in lies,
Or being hated, don't give way to hating,
And yet don't look too good nor talk too
    wise:

If you can dream and not make dreams your
    master,
If you can think and not make thoughts your
    aim,
If you can meet with triumph and disaster,
And treat those two imposters just the same;

If you can bear to hear the truth you've
    spoken
Twisted by knaves to make a trap for fools,
Or watch the things you gave your life to
    broken,
And stoop and build them up with worn out
    tools;

If you can make one heap of all your
    winnings,
And risk it on one turn of pitch-and-toss,
And lose, and start again at your beginnings,
And never breathe a word about your loss;

If you can force your heart and nerve and
    sinew,
To serve your turn long after they are gone,
And so hold on when there is nothing in you
Except the will which says to them:
    "Hold on!"

If you can talk with crowds and keep your
    virtue,
Or walk with kings — not lose the common
    touch.
If neither foes not loving friends can hurt you,
If all men count with you, but none too
    much;

If you can fill the unforgiving minute
With sixty seconds' worth of distance run,
Yours is the Earth and everything that's in it,
And—which is more—you'll be a Man, my
    Son!

Preface

The only thing that I know for sure, is that I know nothing.
— Author Unknown

"For a subject that has been worked and reworked so often in novels, motion pictures and television, American Indians are the least understood and the most misunderstood American of us all."
— President John F. Kennedy, 1963

Truth and Knowledge

The more you know, the more you realize there is to know. Our spectrum of knowledge is exploding exponentially as the Hubble telescope and NASA explore the vast mysteries of the galaxy and microscopes probe the infinitesimal secrets of the DNA helix and genetics. The light of knowledge morphs the truth as we have known it.

The human knowledge curve was a relative flat line for centuries. A hundred years ago, the curve began a steady but relatively flat incline; during the last 20 years the curve has become nearly vertical and we have compiled more knowledge than all of recorded history! What will the knowledge curve look like in the next 10 or 20 years? In the next 100 years? We'll probably need a new frame of reference.

There are very few absolutes in this life. The truth yesterday is not necessarily the truth today, and the truth today may not be the truth tomorrow. Truth is neither black nor white but ever changing shades of gray, depending on the body of knowledge at the time.

The truth is a blend of knowledge and perception that is generally a believable premise or opinion by someone — we consider a knowledgeable expert witness, even though that perception may be flawed by disinformation and/or misinformation. Truth and knowledge are strange companions because one often makes a liar of the other.

Degrees of Truth

Scientific truth — encompasses the laws of nature, physics and mathematics. The development of technology is accelerating scientific discovery at an astounding rate.

Manipulated truth — clever lawyers, politicians and public relations people can manipulate facts to create their particular "spin" and impose their perceptions. If you don't think the truth can be manipulated, listen to opposing trial lawyers or a political debate.

Traditional truth — the things we were taught and believed as children often based on family superstitions, myths and rumor. Memories of scary stories told around the campfire in the woods still affect my thinking.

Deliberate illusion — We live in a world of illusion. Movies, DVDs and television are constructed illusions connected by scenes of scripted human emotions. The line between contrived reality and animation becomes less discernible as technology develops.

People in the entertainment business are already replacing costly movie sets and scenes with realistic video animation. Animation electrodes are being used to electronically simulate the realistic body movements of famous athletes and celebrities. We are on the threshold of improved animation to the degree that most people will not be able to tell the difference between real people and animated people.

Perception of Truth

Each person's truth is their perception of reality. Once perceptions are accepted as fact and are indelibly etched in the subconscious, it is a very difficult process to change those perceptions. The truth can be obiliterated by perception to the extent that perception drives reality.

Even when perceptions are confronted by irrefutable evidence and facts, there is still a time warp between conscious knowledge and subconscious acceptance. The truth becomes a blend of knowledge and perception complicated by what people want to believe and often suits their agenda.

Indian PR & Perception

American Indians have always had a serious public relations problem. By 1890, the last of the Indian wars in the West were over and the battered survivors were herded onto desolate reservations. Spearheaded by pulp novels and western movies, Indians became a blur of monosyllabic drunken savages, living in teepees, usually in a feathered headdress complete with war paint, dancing and whooping around a fire.

They were the hapless victims of a one-sided media campaign that relentlessly created stereotypical images primarily for entertainment. The character assassination was complete to the last detail. America embraced the fictional image to the degree that new myths were created based on old myths. Psychologically, a sub-human savage Indian image was necessary to sanction conquest and soothe the moral conscience of an explosive developing nation.

As a result, the Indian is a historical icon of the past, the villainous savages in John Wayne movies, comedic trivialization, or worse, today as sports teams and their mascots. The best image Indians could hope for was a "Tonto" or "Little Beaver," as trusted companions to their superior white counterparts. Time and technology have desensitized America and provided convenient amnesia to a dark page in America's history.

Contemporary Indian people have become invisible in the mind's eye of the nation's moral conscience. America's conscience has been appeased with regard to the Indian condition by misinformation, disinformation and complacency. When there is reference to minorities, the focus is on African-Americans, Hispanics, Asians and "others." Indian people are usually included among the "others."

Many of us will remember John F. Kennedy, Marilyn Monroe and James Dean as young and vibrant. The reality is that John F. Kennedy would have been 86 years old this year; Marilyn Monroe would have been 78 and James Dean would have been 72. Can you picture any of these people at those ages as they would appear today? In our mind's eye these images are frozen in time.

The American Indian image is also frozen in a historical time warp. Generally speaking, Indian people are usually perceived as icons of the past while current information about today's population, tribes and reservations is essentially ignored.

The Facts of Life

A primary mission of this book is to change the public perception about *today's* American Indians by presenting a compilation of the contemporary facts of life.

Before we can begin to understand Indian people and their issues, it is essential to know the answers to some very basic demographic questions:

❖ What is the Indian population in the United States?
❖ How many tribes exist?
❖ How many reservations are there?

The answers to each of these seemingly simple questions are vast and inherently complex. The true answers lie buried beneath an avalanche of historical distortion, political manipulation and public perception.

Before we engage in this statistical compilation, remember Mark Twain's sage caveat: "There are 3 kinds of lies: there's lies, damned lies and statistics."

Demographics are certainly not an exact science but they are the best information we have as a basis for historical analysis and future projections.

As the Internet develops and becomes the primary repository of human knowledge, it provides instant access to demographic data. The Census 2000 website has a United States and World population clock that provides a daily count. The time lapse between demographic compilation and access on the Internet is diminishing by the minute.

A Matter of Semantics

Over the years, I have been asked hundreds of times what do you want to be called: "Indian," or "American Indian" or "Native American?" (There is also a second tier host of other names: "First Americans," "Native People," etc.) My response was always the same: "I'm a Saginaw Chippewa."

Racial identity was not an issue with Indian people because they inherently self-identified with their respective tribes. From the arrival of Columbus to World War II, the Indian public persona and identity has always been controlled and defined by others.

A rather "thorny" issue in Indian Country: What is the politically correct collective racial identity for Indian people? Shouldn't the people have the right to self-identity?

- ❖ The people were "Indians" from 1492 until World War II.
- ❖ After considerable distinction in World War II, they became "American Indians."
- ❖ During the turbulent 1960s, they became "Native Americans."

How important is it to agree on a collective racial designation? There are 563 federally recognized tribes, more than 40 state-recognized tribes and some 200 unrecognized tribes. If Indian people could agree on what to call themselves collectively, it would make a strong statement for a *self-declared* national identity and enhance the chances for the successful development of cohesive national organizations to address social, political and economic issues. A collective name would help eliminate one basic issue of confusion for everyone.

Indian people are experiencing the same semantic evolution as other ethnic groups. Black people have become African-Americans. Mexicans and Chicanos have become Hispanic and Latino. Chinese, Koreans, Vietnamese, etc. have become American Asians.

The difference between Indians and the other ethnic groups is that Indians were pre-Columbus, pre-America and pre-United States. Indians were the indigenous inhabitants thousands of years before it was America. So defining Indians by an "American" frame of reference seems incongruous at best.

However, "Indian" was never contested for all the obvious reasons and became the accepted designation by America, the world and the Indians themselves.

❖ "Indian" was a misnomer that was accepted as a matter of course for 500 years. Columbus thought he had landed in the East Indies and called the native inhabitants "Indians." (The name "Indian" theoretically, historically and logically belongs to the people of India and the East Indies.)

❖ As the population of people of India descent in the United States increases there is a conflict because they call themselves American Indians. A looming issue is further confusion and conflict on the Internet. (When I do a search for "Indian" or "American Indian," a significant number of the listings are related to people from India, their organizations and businesses.)

❖ "Native American" has gained acceptance in the academic community and seems to be preferred by younger generations.

The term "Native American" came into usage in the 1960s to denote the groups served by the Bureau of Indian Affairs: American Indians and Alaska Indians (Indians, Eskimos and Aleuts of Alaska). The Eskimos and Aleuts in Alaska are two culturally distinct groups and are sensitive about being included under the "Indian" designation. They prefer "Alaska Indian." Later the term also included Indian Hawaiians and Pacific Islanders in Federal programs.

Around 1990, as I became more involved with Indian organizations and activities, I was able to make the transition from "Indian" to "American Indian." It wasn't that much of a stretch and I made the change without much difficulty. Becoming a "Native American" will be much more of a challenge because it sounds antiseptic, plastic and contrived. It implies Indian people's existence began with the discovery of America.

There is also the issue of being an "Indian" (which is grammatically correct and definitive with regard to blood quantum and tribal affiliation), and being "Indian," which is a mindset and a state of being. Personally, I was born "Indian" and I believe that I will always subconsciously think of myself as "Indian."

To further muddy the waters, Census 2000 now includes a Latin American Indian Tribe category as one of the ten largest tribes. Recently, newspaper articles are referring to "Mexican Indians" and "Asian Indians."

American Indian is subconsciously institutionalized by Indian tribes and organizations, the United States government including the Bureau of Indian Affairs, the Indian Health Service, etc., and the public in general. We will fight this battle another day because there are more important issues that need attention and resolution than to be politically correct at this time.

For our purposes, we will use "Indian" and "American Indian" interchangeably and leave the politically correct semantics to the academic community and future generations.

Indian Renaissance

For the first time in history, Indian people have a window of opportunity opened by visibility and resources to create and present their own narrative.

Public libraries, university libraries and museums contain thousands of resources that chronicle every aspect of the fascinating epic as two conflicting cultures engaged in a violent and savage struggle for survival. For Indian people, the struggle continues.

About The Author

Fresh off the Rez

George Russell on the farm at about 10 years old. (We were so poor that we had to borrow the cat from a neighbor for this picture.)

I was born on the Isabella Indian Reservation near Mt. Pleasant, Michigan. We left the reservation when I was about nine years old and moved to the small town of Dansville, Michigan, where I grew up on a small dairy farm. Dairy farming by its nature develops a strong work ethnic and an inherent basic understanding of the close harmony between nature's elements, the land and animals. I was the first in my family to graduate from high school and attend college.

After discharge from the United States Army, I moved to Phoenix, Arizona, where I worked for Consulting Engineers as an interstate highway designer for a few years. I then acquired a General Engineering contractor's license and installed underground utilities and built roads for 20 years.

I consider myself, at best, a pseudo-intellectual with plagiaristic tendencies and a fairly well developed case of Obsessive Compulsive Disorder. I'm also spiritually agnostic and rather short-suited with regard to religion and culture. These characteristics and life experiences have developed a pragmatic personality. Each of us brings different talents and life experiences to the table and each of us have a job to do using those talents.

My primary function is to bridge the gap between the academic community and the general public by compiling and presenting information in a clear, easy-to-use format that will be instrumental in the formation of a realistic perception of American Indians and their issues.

Secondly, to demonstrate what is possible, make it believable and present the viable options to realistically formulate solutions to address Indian issues and problems.

I am an enrolled member of the Saginaw Chippewa Tribe and have lived long enough to be considered a tribal elder with some sense of history.

I am not controlled by any agency or organization and the views expressed are my own. I owe allegiance to no one except my tribe and the Indian people.

I do not ask that you agree with my thoughts and opinions, I only ask that you consider them in your thinking. I hope to include a bit of humor and hopefully will raise more questions than answers.

Thoughts About Truth

Every human being has their moments of truth. Albeit morality, courage or intellect. How we react to those moments of truth tells us who we are in our quiet times. Are we brave and courageous by ourselves or is a matter of conditioning and bravado? Do we have the conviction of our morals or do we weaken under peer pressure and temptation? If left to our own devices, with or with-out acknowledgement and observation, how do we perform?

A holiday is a gift of time, and so for me, everyday's a holiday.

And when you have reached the mountain top,
Then shall you begin to climb,
And when the earth shall claim your limbs,
Then shall you truly dance.

— The inscription on a bench
on a mountaintop in the
Phoenix Mountains in Arizona.

Introduction

The Mission

Our primary Mission is to change the general perception of today's American Indians through education by presenting the facts of life:

❖ A body of demographic information about population, tribes and reservations that will present a "big picture" frame of reference.

❖ Secondly, to organize that demographic data into three easy-to-use resources:

— The *"American Indian Facts of Life"* Handbook.
— The *"Reservations"* Map.
— The *"Native Data"* website (*www.nativedata.com*).

There is a Study Guide near the end of this book. When the reader can answer most of the 38 questions, they will know more about American Indians than 99.9% of the general public. And hopefully, the reader will also be motivated to further study and research in their area of interest.

The Vision

The vision is that the Native Data website *www.nativedata.com* will develop as a major economical and political communications network by linking to every tribal website in the country. *A powerful feature of this forum is that the tribes will control their own information.* Approximately 160 existing tribal websites are linked to the Native Data website and there are plans to build template websites for the approximately 400 remaining tribes.

Research Reference

A few years ago, the research for the map and book was compiled mostly from public libraries, museum libraries and agency reports.

Most of the original research reports and lists are no longer available in print. The revisions and updated information for this printing are compiled primarily from the Internet. The Internet provides instant access to information that pours in faster than it can be assimilated. It's like trying to drink from a fire hose.

In the foreseeable future, the Internet will be the repository for all human knowledge that will be accessible from anywhere on the planet.

We have linked to sites that enhance or contain information we feel is relative. (See the Bibliography for listings.)

Global Perspective

As we begin a new millennium, we can only wonder what the American Indian experience will be 100 years from now. The world is moving at "internet speed" and concern with Indian issues will diminish in direct proportion to the speed of change. Congress simply does not have the time, information or inclination to deal with Indian issues.

Star Trek and space shuttles have let us peek into the foreseeable future as scientists systematically explore the galaxy. Moon explorations are becoming routine. NASA space programs are already busy designing space stations. The United States has robotic vehicles exploring Mars and the Hubble telescope has delivered stunning images of galaxies that existed only in the imagination of human genius.

Are other planets inhabitable? Is there intelligent life on these planets? What effect will these answers have on our religious beliefs? It is presumptuous and arrogant for us to assume that we are the only intelligent life in a universe that, as Carl Sagan succinctly reminded us, has "billions and billions" of planets. Scientific discovery will affect the life of every person on this planet.

Space explorations are the launching pads for a quantum leap in global perception and evolution. We've seen the space photos of Earth that looks like a giant blue and white marble suspended in space. The Moon has changed from a globe of romantic mystique to dusty volcanoes and static human voices. The stars have changed from twinkling points of light to planets ringed by colorful planes of dust and matter.

Computers, the Internet and cost-effective wireless telecommunications have transformed our world into a global community and a global market. Competitive participation is mandatory in the global market for national economic survival. Business is conducted internationally almost as easily as domestic transactions. Internet email gives us access to instant communication with anyone in the world for the price of our local phone service.

A good indicator of the global market impact is the effort to implement the metric system in the United States. The United States has been flirting with the metric system for 30 years and is the only industrialized nation in the world not using the metric system.

Technology, especially the Internet, is the power behind the electronic bullet train of change. The existing socioeconomic gap between American Indians and the rest of society widens in direct proportion to the speed of change. However, there is an incubating Indian Renaissance that could narrow that gap.

"Before we can set out on the road to success, we have to know where we are going, and before we can know that — we must determine where we have been in the past. It seems a basic requirement to study the history of our Indian people. America has much to learn about the heritage of our American Indians. Only through this study can we as a nation do what must be done if our treatment of the American Indian is not to be marked down for all time as a national disgrace."

— President John F. Kennedy, 1963

Section 1:
The Past

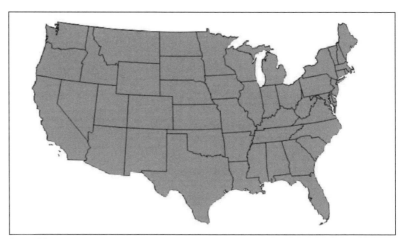

In 1492, historians estimate the population in North America ranged between 5–18 million native people.

1492: Arrival of Columbus

There is considerable speculation with regard to the origin and timeline of the arrival of the Indian people to the continent. Theories are being studied that suggests Indian people's history may be much older than has been generally accepted and they may be the descendants from multiple crossings of several different racial groups. Anthropologic discovery based on new technology will substantiate or dismiss these theories.

The prevalent theory is that at least 12,000 years ago, Indian ancestors crossed the frozen Bering Straits land bridge, fanned out from Alaska and evolved into civilizations on two continents.

Indian people also have their own versions of origin and time.

From the arrival of Columbus to the present, the truth about the Indian people has been obscured by myth and misconception. In 1492, Columbus accidentally landed in the Caribbean Islands while seeking a new trade route to the Far East.

We were taught in school that Christopher Columbus discovered America. The truth is that Columbus never set foot on the con-

tinent we know as America. Explorer Amerigo Vespucci was officially recognized for discovering and naming the Americas.

America was already discovered. Aztec, Mayan, Mound
Builders, Pueblos and numerous other Indian civilizations were
comparable, and in some respects superior, to the contemporary
civilizations in Europe.

Columbus was probably not even the first to explore the New
World. An interesting book titled: *"Columbus Was Last"* by author
Patrick Hughey, offers the compelling premise that there were some
15–20 substantial foreign contacts prior to the arrival of Columbus.

Regardless of the circumstances, the arrival of Columbus to
the New World was a historical accomplishment that initiated a
chain of events that changed the world forever.

Columbus was convinced that he had landed in the East
Indies, an India province, and called the native inhabitants "Indians."
The "Indian" misnomer has been accepted to the extent that it is syn-
onymous with all indigenous people in the Western Hemisphere.

The "Indian" misnomer has been accepted to the extent that it is synonymous with all indigenous people in the western hemisphere.

"Manifest Destiny" & "Divine Providence"

Most Indians view the arrival of Columbus as the beginning
of a 400-year cycle of disease, exploitation, enslavement and genocide that devastated them as a race of people. We can only specu-
late about the massive number of Indian people essentially exterminated by the attrition of genocide for 400 years. The ramifications
of those sustained extermination policies exist today as shortened
life expectancy due to emotional and health problems.

After initial fears had subsided, most Indian people were curi-
ous and even friendly toward the strange invaders. Ironically, some
eastern tribes helped settlers survive the first critical winters. However, conflict between settlers and Indian people was inevitable
because their value system was simply not compatible with that of
the settlers.

By His EXCELLENCY

WILLIAM SHIRLEY, Efq;

Captain-General and Governor in Chief, in and over His Majefty's Province of the *Maffachufetts-Bay*, in *New-England*, and Vice-Admiral of the fame, and Major-General in His Majefty's Army.

A PROCLAMATION.

  HEREAS the Indians of *Norridgewock, Arrefagun a ook, Wewecnock* and *St. John's* Tribes, and the Indians of the other Tribes inhabiting in the Eaftern and Northern Parts of His Majefty's Territories of *New-England*, the Penobfcot Tribe only excepted, have, contrary to their folemn Submiffion unto His Majefty long fince made and frequently renewed, been guilty of the moft perfidious, barbarous and inhuman Murders of divers of h.s Majefty's *Englifh* Subjects ; and have abftained from all Commerce and Correfpondence with His Majefty's faid Subjects for many Months paft ; and the faid *Indians* have fully difcovered an inimical, traiterious and rebellious Intention and Difpofition ;

I have therefore thought fit to iffue this Proclamation, and to Declare the Indians of the Norridgewock, Arrefaguntacook, Wewecnock and St. John's Tribes, and the Indians of the other Tribes new or late inhabiting in the Eaftern and Northern Parts of His Majefty's Territories of New-England, and in Alliance and Confederacy with the above-recited Tribes, the Penobfcots only excepted, to be enemies, Rebels and Traitors to his Moft Sacred Majefty: And I do hereby require his Majefty's Subjects of this Province to embrace all Opportunities of purfuing, captivating, killing and deftroying all and any of the aforefaid Indians, the Penobfcots excepted.

AND WHEREAS the General Court of this Province have voted, That a Bounty or Encouragement be granted and allowed to be paid out of the Publick-Treafury to the marching Army that fhall be employed for the Defence of the Eaftern and Weftern Frontiers from the Twenty-fifth of this Month of *June* until the Twenty-fifth of *November* next ;

I have thought fit to publifh the fame ; and I do hereby promife, That there fhall be paid out of the Province-Treafury to all and any of the faid forces, over and above their Bounty upon Enliftment, their Wages and Subfiftence, the Premiums or Bounties following, viz.

For every Male Indian Prifoner above the Age of Twelve Years, that fhall be taken and brought to *Bofton, Fifty Pounds.*

For every Male Indian Scalp, brought in as Evidence of their being killed, *Forty Pounds.*

For every Female Indian Prifoner, taken and brought in as aforefaid, and for every Male Indian Prifoner under the Age of Twelve Years, taken and brought in as aforefaid, *Twenty-five Pounds.*

For every Scalp of fuch Female Indian or Male Indian under Twelve Years of Age, brought as Evidence of their being killed, as aforefaid, *Twenty Pounds.*

GIVEN under my Hand at Bofton, in the Province aforefaid, this Twelfth Day of June, 1755, *and in the Twenty-eighth Year of the Reign of our Sovereign Lord* GEORGE *the Second, by the Grace of* GOD, *of* Great-Britain, France, *and* Ireland, KING, Defender of the Faith, &c.

By His Excellency's Command,
J. WILLARD, Secr'y.

W. Shirley.

GOD Save the *KING.*

BOSTON: Printed by John Draper, Printer to His ' the Honourable His Majefty's COUNCIL. 1755.

In 1755, the British crown offered 40 pounds for Indian male scalps and 20 pounds for females and children.

Many Indian tribes had developed nomadic lifestyles that were in harmony with the seasons and environment. Their lifestyles were in direct conflict with the fixed homesteads, farms and industrial activity of the European settlers.

The concept of individual land ownership was alien to Indian people. They believed the environmental elements were inseparable and could not be owned by individuals. How can you own the land any more than you can own the sky or the water? Their high regard for the environment was reflected by the inclusion of the elements in most religious ceremonies. The concept of Mother Earth and some special features of the land such as mountains are considered sacred. The issue was compounded by the idea that land ownership could be transferred by a piece of paper.

Settlers felt the Indian people did not make good use of the land and should yield to people who would use the land for more productive purposes. The settlers rationalized that Indian people had no moral right to obstruct the expansion of a higher civilization. Settlers adopted doctrines of "manifest destiny" and "divine providence" as they moved steadily westward.

Settlers adopted doctrines of "manifest destiny" and "divine providence" as they moved steadily Westward.

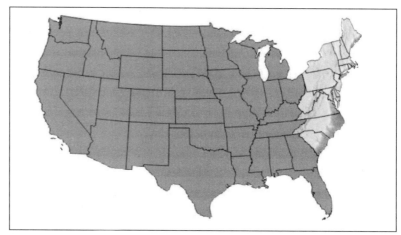

By 1790, the population of the United States was 4 million.

1790: Indians Forced Inland

> *"We the people of the United States, in order to form a more perfect Union, establish justice, insure domestic tranquility, provide for the common defense, promote the general welfare, and secure the blessings of liberty to ourselves and our posterity, do ordain and establish this Constitution for the United States of America."*
>
> — Preamble to the Constitution, 1776

For more than 100 years, European nations made sporadic attempts to establish settlements along the Eastern seaboard. The first permanent settlement was Jamestown, an English colony established in 1607. The Pilgrims landed at Plymouth Rock in 1620. As other colonies were established, settlers began an aggressive policy of expansion by attrition.

Indian tribes finally began to resist with open hostility. The first major retaliation occurred in 1622, when Powhatan leader Opechancanough went on a rampage in Virginia and killed 347 settlers. The conflict initiated a pattern of reciprocal atrocities that lasted for nearly 300 years.

By 1671, there were 50,000 settlers in the Colonies.

By the time the settlers were entrenched along the eastern seaboard, resentment and antagonism toward Indian tribes had escalated. They were considered a sub-human race that must be removed or exterminated. The prevalent attitude tolerated and encouraged the practices of genocide and slavery.

During this same period of time, Spanish encroachment was taking place along the West coast and in the Southwest. Indian people were brutalized and killed with impunity because they did not have a basis for legal recognition or recourse in the country. Indian people could not bear witness against a white man in a court of law. Indian people were not categorically granted citizenship until the Indian Citizenship Act in 1924.

During certain times, many colonies, states and territories paid bounties for the extermination of Indian people. Bounties varied from $25 to $130 for each male scalp and usually half of that amount for women and children. "The only good Indian is a dead Indian" and "nits become lice" were typical expressions that reflected attitudes that lasted for 400 years.

The 1744 Treaty of Lancaster established the Appalachian Mountains as the physical boundary between the settlers and Indian tribes. This general boundary was reaffirmed geographically when the 13 Colonies won their war for independence and became the United States of America.

As settlers' numbers multiplied, their insatiable demand for land forced Indian tribes westward as they fought a losing battle for territory and survival. The conflicts became a war of bizarre perpetual retaliations. Historical records implicate both sides as participants in macabre atrocities.

Bounties varied from $25 to $130 for each male scalp and usually half of that amount for women and children.

Many tribes were essentially wiped out by the thousands. In some instances, the devastation was so complete that pious settlers considered the epidemics as "divine providence."

However, most Indian fatalities were caused by diseases rather than by warfare. Indian people had little immunity to European diseases that were introduced to them as a matter of course, but sometimes by design.

Smallpox, cholera, malaria, syphilis and influenza are a few of the diseases that decimated the Indian population. Many tribes were essentially wiped out by the thousands. In some instances, the devastation was so complete that pious settlers considered the epidemics "divine providence."

Survivors of disease and genocide were subject to the widespread practice of slavery. Indian people were sold as slaves to work plantations and mines. Conquest has been standard operating procedure since man became "civilized" even among Indian tribes. The victims of conquest suffer "man's inhumanity to man." Indian tribes practiced bondage and other atrocities as rituals of intertribal warfare for centuries. However, the white slave traders escalated the practice to the scale of commercial enterprise.

In 1829, the population of the United States was 12.5 million.

1830: Indian Country

The 1830 Indian Removal Act, signed into law by President Andrew Jackson, extinguished Indian tribal land rights east of the Mississippi. It provided for their relocation to "Indian Country," which was defined as "the part of the United States West of the Mississippi and not within the states of Missouri, Louisiana or the territory of Arkansas."

This definitive boundary seemed to create a brief pause in the settlers' voracious appetite for Indian tribal lands. However, an ominous tidal wave of immigrants was building along the western frontier.

Equal integration seems to require a more resolute will from some racial groups than others.

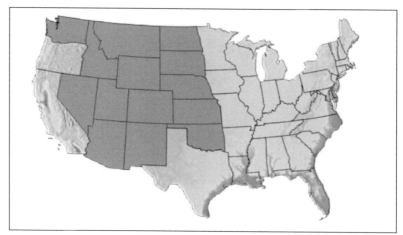

By 1860, the population of the United States was 31 million.

1860: Immigrant Stampede

"I am tired of fighting. Our chiefs are killed. It is cold and we have no blankets. The little children are freezing to death. Hear me, my chiefs, I am tired, my heart is sick and sad. From where the sun now stands I will fight no more forever."
— Nez Perce Chief Joseph, 1877

By 1850, the United States had extinguished all European land claims from coast to coast, setting the stage for the settlement of the West. Only the Indian tribes stood in the way of progress.

The 1854 Indian Appropriation Act gave Congress the authority to establish Indian Reservations. The act provided the legal basis for removal of specific Indian tribes to specific locations. In 1862, President Lincoln signed the Homestead and Railroad Acts into law which became major factors in crushing Indian tribal resistance.

The discovery of gold in the West and availability of free land launched a stampede of humanity across the land. When the dust settled, Indian tribal land rights had essentially been extinguished and the devastated Indian people had nearly been exterminated. In the wake of this carnage, the western half of a new nation was born.

A case in point: In the early 1800s, there were an estimated 260,000 Indian people in California: by 1900, there were 20,000 survivors.

By 1890, the population of the United States was 63 million. Indians on reservations were included for the first time in the 1890 Census. The Indian population was 237,000.

Treaties were interpreted to Indian tribal leaders who rarely knew what was actually written on the document placed before them for mark or signature.

1890: The Vanquished Indian

By 1890, the last of the Indian wars were over, and the 1887 Indian Dawes Allotment Act was the *"coup de grace"* for Indian tribal land rights. The essence of this act was to eliminate the rights of Indian people to hold tribal land in common. Those rights were exchanged for individualized allotments of 160 acres per head of household, with lesser acreages to individuals. The 1860 surplus land was ceded to the government and sold to the settlers. More than 100 reservations were allotted and over 90 million acres were abstracted from Indian lands.

The 1887 Dawes Act, the 1934 Indian Reorganization Act, the 1954 Termination & Relocation Act, etc. were supposedly well-intentioned legislation to remedy past wrongs and help Indian people toward prosperity and independence. However, when the dust

It seems that Indian people have been harmed as much by good intentions as by bad intentions. Although the bad intentions were more direct and brutal, the results are the same.

settled at the end of each act's tenure, the bottom line was that Indian people had less than when they started.

It seems that Indian people have been harmed as much by good intentions as by bad intentions. Although the bad intentions were more direct and brutal, the results are the same.

In fewer than 100 years, Indian tribal lands had been reduced from all land west of the Appalachian Mountains to desolate reservations totaling less than four percent of the continental United States.

During the development of America, tremendous hardships were endured by immigrants of all races. There has always been a "pecking order" as each new ethnic group struggled to overcome racial prejudice and weave their particular talents into the fabric of America. Equal integration seems to require a more resolute will from some racial groups than others.

Indian tribes fought for their inalienable aboriginal land rights. The fierce resistance resulted in 400 years of Indian bashing that left a physically deteriorated people with deep psychological wounds. Indian people had lost their land, self-image, self-esteem and were rapidly becoming a vanishing race.

Ironically, during intense oppression of the Indian people, the United States fought the Revolutionary War for freedom and independence. The Emancipation Proclamation, President Lincoln's declaration to free the black race from slavery, was a cornerstone of the Civil War. These lofty ideals were to establish the moral fiber and political creed of the United States.

The rhetorical question is, "Could the Indian people dilemma have been resolved in a more humane and equitable manner?" Probably not, within the context of the times.

> *"We hold these truths to be self-evident, that all men are created equal, that they are endowed by their Creator with certain unalienable Rights, that among these are Life, Liberty and the pursuit of Happiness."*
> — Declaration of Independence, 1776

Chronology from 1492 to the present

This abbreviated list of historical events significantly influenced the course of Indian destiny and provides a chronological timeline.

1492	Arrival of Columbus to the New World.
1607	Jamestown was founded.
1620	Pilgrims land at Plymouth Rock.
1622	First major Indian retaliation.
1744	The Treaty of Lancaster.
1775	American Revolutionary War begins.
1776	Declaration of Independence.
1778	First treaty between United States & Indians.
1783	American Revolutionary War ends.
1803	Louisiana purchased for $15 million.
1824	BIA established under Department of War.
1830	Indian Removal Act.
1848	First gold strike in California.
1850	United States eliminates all foreign land claims.
1854	Indian Appropriation Act.
1861	Civil War begins.
1862	Railroad Act.
1865	Civil War ends.
1868	Fort Laramie peace conference.
1871	Treaties end between United States & Indians.
1887	General Allotment Act. (Dawes Act)
1917	United States Enters World War I.
1919	Treaty of Versailles ends World War I.
1924	Indian Citizenship Act.
1934	Indian Reorganization Act.
1941	United States Enters World War II.
1944	National Congress of American Indians Organized.
1945	World War II ends with the atomic bomb.
1947	Indian Claims Commission Act.

As ludicrous as it may sound, American Indians were categorically granted United States citizenship by the 1924 Indian Citizenship Act.

Treaties became the legal basis used by encroaching settlers to appropriate Indian tribal lands.

1948	Indians allowed to vote in Arizona.
1953	Liquor Prohibition repealed for Indians.
1954	Termination & Relocation Act.
1962	Indians allowed to vote in New Mexico.
1968	Indian Civil Rights Act.
1972	Indian Education Act.
1975	Indian Self-Determination & Education Assistance Act.
1978	American Indian Religious Freedom Act.
1978	Indian Child Welfare Act.
1988	Indian Gaming Regulatory Act.
1990	Indian Arts & Crafts Act.
1990	Native American Graves Protection & Repatriation Act
1992	Indian Languages Act.
2001	The Destruction of the World Trade Center on Sept. 11, 2001.

Groundless treaties

Because Indian tribes were the sole inhabitants of the North American continent, it was imperative for European nations to establish a legal concept of aboriginal land rights as a basis for treaty negotiations. Treaties became the legal basis used by encroaching settlers to appropriate Indian tribal lands.

Typical treaty negotiations were based on huge Indian tribal land cessions in exchange for reservation areas, food, hardware goods and annuity payments. During the translation from document to reality, questionable sincerity succumbed to avarice and self-serving rationalization. The government's "perpetual guaranty" of Indian tribal lands did not endure, and the delivery of food, goods and monies failed to match the promises.

Indian tribes were at a distinct disadvantage during treaty negotiations because the treaty documents were written in a language

Indian people did not understand. Treaties were interpreted to Indian tribal leaders who rarely knew what was actually written on the document placed before them for mark or signature. Other ruses included negotiation of a treaty with a manageable Indian who did not represent the tribe or plying the negotiators with whiskey.

Hundreds of treaties were negotiated between Indian tribes and European settlers from early colonial days to the establishment of the United States. In 1778, the United States government entered into its first official treaty with the Delaware. At least 370 documented treaties were negotiated and ratified by Congress during the next 100 years.

In 1871, Congress declared that no Indian nation would be recognized for the purpose of making treaties. By then, Indian tribes realized that treaty negotiations had become a charade of empty promises based on fraud and deceit for the convenience of the government and the benefit of the land-hungry settlers.

An inherent stipulation in these treaty negotiations was the trust responsibility of the United States government to provide for the health, education and entitlement of the Indian people. The general consensus in the Indian community is that government has not lived up to its trust responsibilities. These issues have not been resolved to an equitable conclusion. Some Indian tribes and organizations are seeking reparations through the legal system.

Any special rights that Indian tribes or members of those tribes have are generally based on treaties or other agreements between the United States and tribes.

Vanquished Indian people

> *"Give me your tired, your poor your huddled masses yearning to breathe free, the wretched refuse of your teeming shore. Send these, the homeless, tempest tossed to me. I lift my lamp beside the golden door."*
> — Statue of Liberty Inscription, 1903

Indian people became a maligned blur of fact and fiction. The movie blitz was so effective that most fictitious perceptions still exist today.

By 1890, the physically battered Indian people were decimated. Those remaining were confined to desolate reservations with their daily regimen of hardships, humiliation and exploitation. The once fearsome warrior had been reduced to a despised beggar, thief and nuisance. The reservation system served to keep Indian people out of sight and under control. Indian tribes essentially became wards of the government, whose needs were given a low priority.

The vanquished Indian tribes became a favorite subject of the media. Their plight was compounded by the invention of motion pictures. The nation's concept of Indian people was the indelible celluloid images created by Hollywood westerns for entertainment. Marauding hordes became villainous savage anti-heroes as they attacked hopelessly outnumbered courageous settlers. Indian people became a maligned blur of fact and fiction. The movie blitz was so effective that most fictitious perceptions still exist today.

In the last few years, movies such as *Dances With Wolves, Black Robe, Thunderheart* and *Incident at Oglala,* have attempted to present a more realistic image and history of Indian people.

Today, a new cadre of talented Indian people in the entertainment industry are creating, organizing and producing their own version of Indian history and stories. Productions about Indian people can never have the innate authenticity of productions by Indian people. Indian people should tell Indian stories.

America's Holocaust

There have been numerous studies regarding the Indian population when Columbus reached the New World. Most studies included North and South America with estimates that ranged from 5 to 30 million

American Indian Holocaust and Survival Population History Since 1492, published in 1987 by author Russell Thornton, is a very interesting definitive study of American Indian population before and after the arrival of Columbus. (Thornton's book is available in most libraries, bookstores and at Amazon.com.)

The consensus is that when the Europeans began to occupy the New World, there were at least 5 million Indian people existing as some 500 tribes ranging in size from a few dozen to several thousand, speaking some 500 languages.

Thornton's hypothesis indicates that there were approximately 5 million Indian people within the continental United States at the arrival of Columbus to the New World. Five million Indian people divided by 500 tribes = 10,000 people average for each tribe. Even with the larger tribes scattered in bands and clans, those are significant tribes. Was there enough food supply to support these numbers?

Two disturbing hypothetical questions come to mind based on Thornton's research:

❖ Assuming there were 5 million Indian people around 1500 the Census Bureau officially counted 237,000 survivors in 1900. How many millions of Indian people were essentially exterminated during a 400-year period, either directly and/or indirectly, as a result of European contact?

❖ Secondly, if the 1492 Indian population of 5 million had continued to increase at a normal rate, what would the Indian population be today?

❖ The Jewish Holocaust of 6 million people is the only event of that magnitude that can begin to be used for comparison and it pales by comparison.

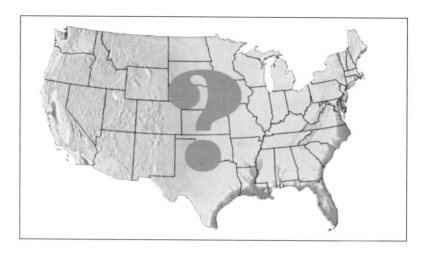

2100: Indian Lands?

"The utmost good faith shall always be observed toward the Indians; their land and property shall never be taken from them without their consent; and in their property, rights and liberty, they shall never be invaded or disturbed, unless in just and lawful wars authorized by Congress; but laws founded on justice and humanity shall from time to time be made, for preventing wrongs done to them, and for preserving peace and friendship with them."
— United States Congress Northwest Ordinance, 1787

Third World conditions are still the
reality for most of Native America and
they are still the poorest race of people
in the country with regard to health,
education and welfare. The prosperity of
a handful of hugely successful gaming
tribes has eclipsed the grinding poverty
of the vast majority of American Indians.

Section 2:
The Facts
of Life

CHAPTER 1 — POPULATION

Statistics and Demographics

Remember Mark Twain's caveat:

"There are three kinds of lies: lies, damned lies and statistics."

The Merriam-Webster dictionary defines **statistics** as a *branch of mathematics dealing with the collection, analysis, interpretation, and presentation of masses of numerical data.*

Demographics *are the statistical characteristics of human populations.*

There are several inherent systemic foibles with statistics and demographics:

❖ If we utilize the best and most recent population statistics available and extrapolate by the best methods possible, *theoretically,* the numbers will be incorrect by the next day, the next week, the next month or the next year because people are born and people die every minute. The Census 2000 website population clock is a ticking reminder of this fact of life.

❖ Most demographics usually have several different sources that may have varying numbers for the same statistic.

❖ After every Decennial Census, there is a flurry of criticism that some people were under-counted and some people were over-counted depending on methodology, motive and agenda.

❖ There is the potential for statistical and demographic manipulation to accommodate the agenda of the people compiling the numbers.

Indian reservations posed problems to Census 2000 takers, not the least of which were large, ever-changing households, frequent moves, mistrust of government officials, and differing definitions of who is an Indian. As a result, the head count of Indians had some of the highest error rates for any minority group in the country.

More than 100 tribes around the country are challenging the 2000 Census results and are conducting their own head counts, hoping ultimately to win more federal money for such things as health care and housing.

According to Donna White, a spokeswoman for the United States Department of Housing and Urban Development, as of November 1, 2003, 78 tribes had completed their recounts and 39 had won challenges to the official numbers.

According to Rick Anderson of Tribal Data Resources, a Redding, California company that is advising tribes, approximately fifty other tribes are conducting or considering their own head counts.

If these statistical compilations are successful and the trend continues, it would be a quantum leap for the tribes to self-generate an accurate head count. It is essential for the tribes to have a forum where they can control and post their own information. This type of endeavor would be a giant step toward tribal self-determination, unity and an exercise of tribal sovereignty. The final step is to organize the data and make it available at an Indian-controlled website such as *www.nativedata.com* or one like it.

Egocentric tribalism and fear of past experiences will make a centralized information center somewhat difficult, but it is definitely within the realm of possibility. The tribes can provide only the information that would be beneficial to their respective tribes.

The benefits of such a forum would far outweigh any negative connotations. Indian tribes have suffered in the past by providing information that was not used in their best interest. Consequently,

There is a generational genetic time-bomb quietly ticking in Indian country; blood quantum.

they are very wary and cautious about releasing internal data. The sovereignty issue also plays a major role in the process.

Before an organization can launch any meaningful campaign, they must know the logistics of their resources. People are the most important resource and voting people are the most important political resource in a democratic society. Everything else is secondary and subsequent. Demographics are an essential element of the democratic process that can be the catalyst to motivate and initiate dialogue that will benefit the long-term future of the Indian people.

Like it or not, demographics are certainly not an exact science but it's the best that we have to work with. Demographics are a reasonable basis to make predictable projections if certain trends continue or a course of action is taken. And the United States Census Bureau has the most resources and the best qualified people to do the job. They haven't got it right yet, but they are getting better at it.

We're using Census 2000 numbers as our primary demographic resource and it's already 2004! Fortunately, the Census Bureau does make certain Press Releases and Reports available between Decennial Census as they become available.

Genetic Roulette

There is a generational genetic time-bomb quietly ticking in Indian country; **blood quantum.** By the end of the 1890s after the Indian tribes were under control, the United States government began a systematic tribal enumeration and classification.

The tribes did not have a choice in the matter and were not in the position to contribute to the system that would control their destiny. And the tribes probably did not have the expertise to make the right choices if they were given the opportunity. Consequently, the tribes unknowingly became passive players in an insidious convoluted game of genetic roulette instituted by the United States government more than 100 years ago when tribes were weak and vulnerable.

The tribes were instructed and coerced into accepting institutionalized blood quantum as the primary requirement for tribal membership. (Perhaps tribal membership could not have been determined any other way.) At the time, tribes were more concerned with survival than the long-term ramifications that the blood quantum criteria for tribal membership would have on future generations.

Theoretically, as the "blooded" elders die, the Indian blood quantum gene pool will become more diluted with each succeeding generation until it is extinguished. This is happening very rapidly to Urban Indians, which constitute 78% of the American Indian population.

Blood quantum may accomplish what diseases, wars and 400 years of genocide failed to achieve.

Definition of a "Legal" Indian:

The United States government's definition of a legal Indian is:

"Any person who has the certifiable Indian blood quantum to meet the enrollment requirements of a federally recognized tribe."

This seemingly innocuous definition has been the cause of enormous dilemma in the Indian communities. Each tribe has the right to determine the minimum blood quantum requirements for enrollment.

At one end of the spectrum: The Cherokee Nation of Oklahoma was one of the first tribes to adopt the liberal policy of linear ancestry documentation as criteria for enrollment. They accept anyone who can trace and document their linear ancestry to the Dawes Commission of Final Rolls compiled between the years of 1899–1906, regardless of blood quantum. Some enrolled Cherokees have a minute trace of Indian blood such as $\frac{1}{512}$ or less. This liberal policy has increased Cherokee Nation of Oklahoma enrollment to more than 300,000. The other Cherokee tribes have more stringent enrollment requirements.

At the other end of the spectrum are the several tribes that still require 1/2 minimum blood quantum for membership.

Approximately 2/3 of the tribes require 1/4 minimum blood quantum, and approximately 1/3 have adopted linear descendants as membership criteria. Indian people are the only race who must legally document that they are Indian. (Other races are accepted at face value. No pun intended.)

Tribal "Full Blood" Indians

The term "full-blood" is a designation that some Indians claim who consider themselves to have 100% blood quantum of one tribe. Is this possible or does "full-blood" at best mean tribal Indian blood? Considering that the inter-tribal melting pot has existed for thousands of years, the designation would seem to be more of a reference to tribal identity, spirituality and culture than definitive tribal blood quantum in its truest sense.

Tribally Hyphenated Indians

Ethnic Groups are groups of people classed according to common racial, national, tribal, religious, linguistic, or cultural origin or background.

Human hybrids are people whose genetic composition is a blend of two or more ethnic groups.

Over the eons as Indian tribes adapted to their geographic environment, distinctive physical features, customs and religions evolved. The West coast tribes looked different from the Eastern tribes; and the Plains tribes looked different from the Southern tribes.

Indian people within geographic areas mixed inter-tribally for thousands of years by natural selection to preclude the contamination of a limited gene pool by genetic inbreeding. Especially within the smaller tribes, cousins could end up marrying cousins within a couple of generations. Trading between friendly tribes within geographic territories were occasions for social interaction and it was accepted custom to seek a mate from a neighboring tribe or clan. The progeny of these customs were integrated into host tribes as accepted members.

Today, there is usually a core population in most tribes that retain the physically distinct features of their respective tribes.

During the 500 years since initial contact with European immigrants and especially the past 200 years, the patterns of Indian tribal natural selection was significantly impacted by the dispossession and relocation mandates of "manifest destiny" and "divine providence."

❖ The 100-year Treaty Era, from 1778 to 1871, had a tremendous affect on tribal hyphenation. Most treaties were one-sided huge land cessions in exchange for territorial reservations supposedly in perpetuity during which Indians were dispossessed and relocated.

❖ Another set of circumstances was the social experiment of the Indian schools. Children were removed from tribal homelands and integrated with children from different tribes in different parts of the country.

❖ After World War II, there was an increase in social acceptance, mobility and education of the veterans.

❖ One last factor, still in its infancy, is the affect on high per capita tribes. Seventy three tribes pay per capita, some modest and some are phenomenal. I constantly hear stories about the schemes and extremes that people employ to marry a per capita tribal member.

The creation of the reservation system and forced relocation of tribes were major factors that accelerated the inter-tribal melting pot.

Pictographs in Arizona. (National Archives)

Animal Skin Pictorial. (National Archives)

Approximately 1/3 of the tribes see the "handwriting on the wall" and have modified their blood quantum requirements to linear descendants. Some tribes have modified their enrollment criteria to accept other composite tribal blood. Tribes do not allow membership in more than one tribe.

There are Indian families who have lived in Indian communities, sometimes for generations, who do not have official records to document blood quantum required for enrollment certification.

Most Indian tribes did not have written languages. During periods of relocation and assimilation, genealogy often became a matter of oral interpretation. Most Indian languages were difficult for Europeans to understand and pronounce, so when the enumerator couldn't pronounce or understand 8 syllable Indian names, the person became John Jackson, Joe Smith, etc. A combination of oral and sign language became the basis for communication. As a result, Indians were often given arbitrary anglicized names for the records.

During World War I and World War II, the Indians volunteered and distinguished themselves in disproportionately large numbers. After World War II, having Indian blood lost some of its stigma and became more socially acceptable. Since the 1990s when Indian casinos began to prosper, the interest in establishing an Indian connection has increased dramatically. Today, it seems that everyone who has a remote Indian ancestor wants to be recognized as an Indian and enrolled if possible.

The result is a pyramid of tribally and racially mixed blood Indian people that grows exponentially with each succeeding generation. Granted, the number of Indians increases as the spectrum of blood quantum decreases.

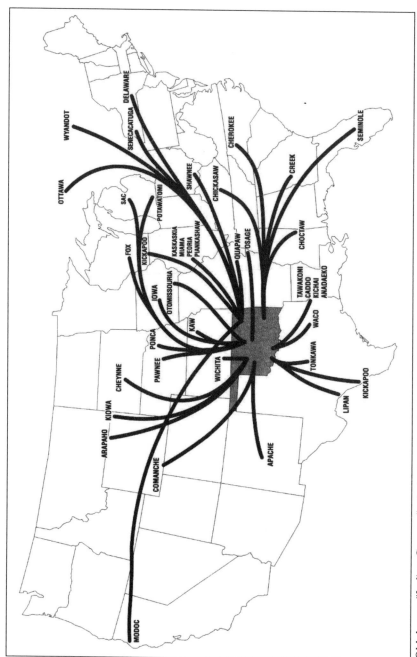

Oklahoma "Indian Country" tribal relocation during the 1800s

Oklahoma Tribal Relocation

The most notorious example was the relocation of some 60 tribes from all parts of the country to Oklahoma territory during the 1800s.

The infamous "Trail of Tears" generally refers to the 1838 forced march of some 15,000 Cherokee people from their homelands in the southeastern United States to Oklahoma Indian territory, during which some 4,000 perished along the way from disease, exposure and starvation.

The Indian Removal Act of 1830 was actually much broader in scope because it lasted for nearly 10 years and when the dust settled, some 60,000 members of the five "Civilized Tribes" had been removed from the southeastern United States to Oklahoma.

The forced removal was in violation of a Supreme Court decision by Chief Justice John Marshall in favor of the Indian people to which President Andrew Jackson responded, "John Marshall has made his decision, now let him enforce it."

The large concentration of other tribes relocated to Oklahoma came from a wide range of geographic areas. Consequently, Oklahoma Indian history presents a much larger view of Indian America than is indicated by the relatively small geographic area.

> "It affords me sincere pleasure to be able to apprise you of the entire removal of the Cherokee Nation of Indians to their new homes West of the Mississippi their removal has been principally under the conduct of their own chiefs, and they have migrated without any apparent reluctance."
> — President Martin Van Buren, 1838

As Senator DeConcini of Arizona so aptly stated from a congressional perspective: "Nobody gives a damn about Indians."

Each Urban American Indian must determine what degree of adaptation is required to function as a productive member of society and yet preserve their American Indian connections.

Racially Hyphenated Indians

Settler, pioneer and frontier life in early America was a perilous regimen of hardships. Consequently, there was an acute shortage of European women. Because of the imbalance, sexual interaction between European men and Indian women was an inevitable and common practice.

On the basis of this premise, there is the strong probability that there is Indian blood in the veins of a much larger segment of the population than was recorded or acknowledged. Since World War II, there is more of an inclination to acknowledge an Indian skeleton in the family closet.

The premise of racial Indian blood mixing can be compared to the African slavery experience and the proliferation of mixed blood children as an aftermath of military occupation in foreign lands. Consensual and non-consensual sexual activity has always been considered a military prerogative during territorial conquest and occupation. "The brotherhood of man" may be a much more appropriate expression than we realize.

Large segments of today's Indians are also racially hyphenated for generations within their geographic regions (Cherokee-Choctaw-Creek-English-Irish-African, etc). These two genetic realities raise some thorny issues. Who is and who isn't Indian, either by legal definition or by self-identification, has become an important issue for Indians and their respective tribes.

Contrary to the stereotypical image, today's Indians come in all sizes, shapes and colors. At any major Pow Wow, conference or trade show, the color spectrum will range from blue-eyed Indians to the African features of the buffalo soldiers and everything in between.

From the turn of the century until World War II, Indians were subjected to the coercion of boarding schools, assimilation and relocation programs. The idea of this period was to civilize Indians by cultural genocide. Richard H. Pratt founded the Carlisle Indian

Industrial School and his mantra was: "kill the Indian and save the child." And Captain Pratt was one of the good guys.

Carlisle Indian School boys, 1880. (National Archives)

Carlisle Indian School boys and girls, 1915. (National Archives)

During World War II, 25,000 Indians left the reservations to serve in the armed forces. After the war, migrations accelerated as Indians sought employment, education and opportunity.

❖ Most Reservation Indians and Urban Indians have close family ties and interact culturally. Many Urban Indians live near their respective reservations.

❖ That core group of enrolled members who live and work on their reservation.

❖ Enrolled members who live and work near their reservation and are still closely connected to family. Some still have a reservation residence.

❖ Geographically relocated enrolled "at large" tribal members.

❖ Most tribes have some community members who are connected by lineal descent or affiliated by marriage but are not enrolled, who are active in the community and consider themselves Indians traditionally and spiritually.

❖ Perhaps the largest group is people who have an Indian ancestor generations removed, but have lost their tribal connection and are not active in the Indian community.

Census 2000

Census 2000 made the effort to do a much better job of counting Indians than in 1990. Partnerships were developed with the Urban and Reservation communities by hiring Indian people as administrators and enumerators to count Indian people.

Census 2000 has muddied the waters of the blood quantum issue further by counting people who consider themselves mixed-bloods of more than one race. These are people who have Indian blood in combination with other races.

❖ 2,476,000 people are self-identified American Indians. Self-identified means there is a box on the Census 2000 form

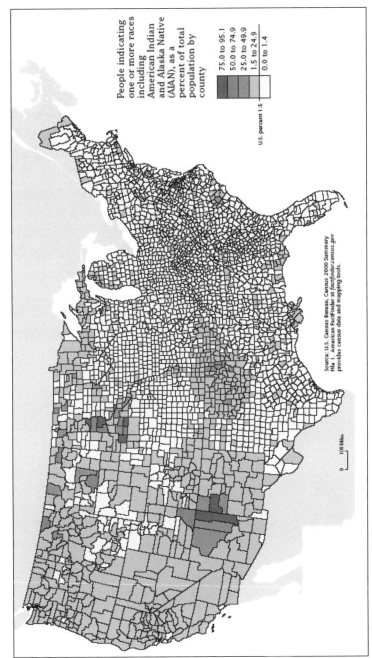

People indicating
one or more races
including
American Indian
and Alaska Native
(AIAN), as a
percent of total
population by
county

75.0 to 95.1
50.0 to 74.9
25.0 to 49.9
1.5 to 24.9
0.0 to 1.4

U.S. percent 1.5

Source: U.S. Census Bureau, Census 2000 Summary
File 1. American FactFinder at factfinder.census.gov
provides census data and mapping tools.

0   100 Miles

Indian population map, Census 2000

that says American Indian if you mark the box, you are counted as Indian. (The Census 2000 form also asks for tribal affiliation which should be very interesting.)

❖ 538,000 Indians live on-reservation. (22% of the total Indian population.)

❖ 1,938,000 Indians live off-reservation. (78% of the total Indian population.)

❖ 1,700,000 of those Indians are enrolled tribal members.

❖ Indicating there are some 776,000 (2,476,000–1,700,000 = 776,000) people who consider themselves Indians and were counted as Indians but are not enrolled members of a tribe.

❖ An additional 1.6 million people believe they have an identifiable Indian ancestor in combination with other 1 or more other races.

❖ Anthropologists estimate there are some 15 million people who believe they have an Indian ancestor but have lost their tribal connection. (I believe the number may be much larger than 15 million.)

Urban Indian Migration		
Year	Indian Population	% Urban
1890	248,000	0
1900	237,000	0
1910	277,000	4
1920	244,000	6
1930	343,000	10
1940	345,000	7
1950	357,000	13
1960	524,000	28
1970	793,000	44
1980	1,364,000	49
1990	1,959,000	65
2000	2,476,000	78

Source: US Census Bureau

Urban Indians

I am not comfortable with the term "Urban" Indians but until there is a better designation, it will have to do. One of the major issues for Urban Indians is tribal members who do not reside on their reservations have limited relations with the Bureau of Indian Affairs (BIA) and Indian Health Service (IHS) because BIA and IHS programs are primarily administered for members who live on or near reservations. And yet off-reservation members are included in the head count as a basis for program funding allocations.

The Indian population is further complicated by the evolution of two more categories: Reservation Indians and Urban Indians (tribal people who live off-reservation). Isn't it ironic that the United States government damned near exterminated the Indians using

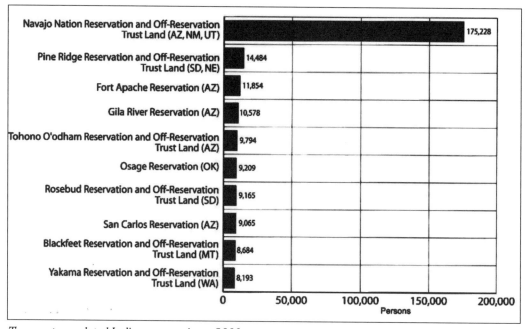

Ten most populated Indian reservations, 2000.

military force to relocate them to their designated reservations; and then spent the next 50 years implementing various programs to get the Indians to leave the reservations!

Indians who are born and become adults on the reservation will generally stay on or near the reservation or return if they leave. For Indians born off-reservation, the chances of returning are remote, especially if the family migration occurred generations ago and if they relocated geographically.

Indian Population by State

Rank	State	Population
1	California	333,000
2	Oklahoma	273,000
3	Arizona	256,000
4	New Mexico	173,000
5	Texas	118,000
6	North Carolina	100,000
7	Alaska	98,000
8	Washington	93,000
9	New York	92,000
10	Michigan	58,000

Source: US Census 2000

Indian Population by City

Rank	State	Population
1	New York City	87,200
2	Los Angeles	53,100
3	Phoenix	35,100
4	Tulsa	30,200
5	Oklahoma City	29,000
6	Anchorage	27,000
7	Albuquerque	22,000
8	Chicago	20,900
9	San Diego	16,200
10	Houston	15,700

Source: US Census 2000

Indian poupulation by United States geographic region.

59

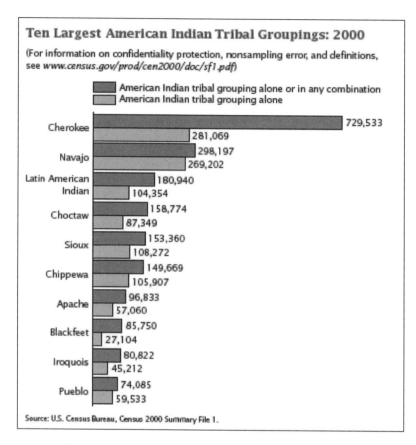

Ten Largest American Indian Tribal Groupings: 2000

(For information on confidentiality protection, nonsampling error, and definitions, see *www.census.gov/prod/cen2000/doc/sf1.pdf*)

■ American Indian tribal grouping alone or in any combination
▨ American Indian tribal grouping alone

Tribe	Alone or in any combination	Alone
Cherokee	729,533	281,069
Navajo	298,197	269,202
Latin American Indian	180,940	104,354
Choctaw	158,774	87,349
Sioux	153,360	108,272
Chippewa	149,669	105,907
Apache	96,833	57,060
Blackfeet	85,750	27,104
Iroquois	80,822	45,212
Pueblo	74,085	59,533

Source: U.S. Census Bureau, Census 2000 Summary File 1.

Are Indian Tribes Programmed for Extinction?

This situation creates an internal dilemma: Reservation Indians receive the direct benefits of federal programs including housing, utility subsidies, health care, education and economic development aid, while their enrolled Urban Indian counterparts are essentially excluded from most of these programs.

There are three critical issues facing Indian America with regard to the population and the continuity of future generations:

❖ The dilution of blood quantum.
❖ Nurture Urban Indian connections.
❖ Loss of tribal language.

Blood quantum is the cause of considerable division and inequities in the Indian community. An example of the extreme blood quantum spectrum: some Oklahoma Cherokees have a minute trace (such as 1/512) of Indian blood and are enrolled tribal members, while other Indians are composite "full-bloods" but are not enrolled because they do not have the documented blood quantum to meet any of their respective tribal requirements.

The tribal hyphenation happens very quickly through tribal inter-marriage.

Theoretically, if a Navajo man marries a Hopi woman;

And their Navajo-Hopi son marries a Sioux-Crow wife;

And their Navajo-Hopi-Sioux-Crow grandson marries a Pima-Kaw-Apache-Ute wife;

Their great-grandchildren are Navajo-Hopi-Sioux-Crow-Pima-Kaw-Apache-Ute.

In four generations, the grandchildren are full-blood Indians with 1/8 blood quantum from 8 different tribes. If all 8 tribes have a 1/4 minimum blood quantum for membership; these direct descendants cannot be members of any of their respective tribes.

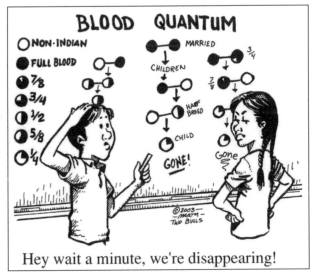

Indian artist Marty Two Bulls, 2003,
Indian Country Today *newspaper*

It is not appropriate, prudent or moral that the children and grandchildren of tribal members are not members of the same tribe as their grandfathers.

There is no solution that will satisfy or include everyone. The cold hard facts of life are that some people are going to be excluded who should be included; and some people will be included who should be excluded. Do the issues have black and white answers, or does the solution lie in the gray area of compromise?

It is not appropriate, prudent or moral that the children and grandchildren of tribal members are not members of the same tribe as their grandfathers. The bottom line is that theoretically, the Indian gene pool will become smaller with each generation until it is extinguished. This is happening very rapidly to Urban Indians, which constitutes 78% of the Census 2000 Indian population. Urban Indians are the largest tribe of all.

Remember that only 22% of the Indian population live on reservations and 78% are Urban Indians. Three out of four Indians do not marry other Indians. Do the math and project those numbers a couple of generations. The vast majority (78%) are being absorbed very rapidly and the 22% will be severely diminished unless some dramatic changes are made.

The question has been asked, "Why don't Indians marry other Indians?" In affairs of the heart and the heat of the moment, young hormones do not have much regard for blood quantum or tribal affiliation.

When tribal people argue internally about who is and who isn't a tribal member, they are unwittingly participating in the United States government strategy of "divide and conquer." Whether by design or attrition, identity politics is an invention of the United States government and its still working very well today. It is foolish and self-defeating to criticize one another for cultural and racial dilution that was initiated by the United States government. In this sense, Indians have become their own worst enemy.

Indian people struggle with the enrollment process to become members of their own tribes, yet they are citizens of the United States simply by being born.

The pendulum has swung from being inclusive (when the United States government and society branded anyone with the slightest Indian connection — similar to the "one-drop doctrine" of slave days) to tribal policies of membership exclusivity because of limited government program resources and gaming benefits. And if Indians are honest with themselves, they will acknowledge that exclusivity is mostly based on greed! Not that a little avarice is a bad thing but it cannot become more important than the continuity of future generations.

Wiser souls must look at the bigger picture, because the short-term benefits are not worth the long-term loss of people. It is human nature, but arrogant, for people to take credit for their birth circumstances. If you are born with blond hair and blue eyes, you had nothing to do with it. Or if you were lucky enough to be born Indian, or born on the reservation, you had absolutely nothing to do with it. Blood quantum is not a matter of choice. It's the luck of the draw.

We are the lucky ones, the ones who by circumstances, not by choice, still have that precious tribal connection: Why would we not be generous and kind by embracing our less fortunate relatives? It's ironic that Indian people who would not yield to the yoke, those who hid in the mountains and were never enrolled for a multitude of reasons, are now the ones excluded.

In order to survive genetically and politically, Indian tribes must develop an inclusive rather than exclusive philosophy and agenda. On a humanitarian or moral basis, no one has the right to deny a person the recognition and acknowledgement of their ancestral origins. Acknowledgment of related people doesn't necessary mean enrollment, it could mean affiliation.

It's ironic that Indian people who would not yield to the yoke, those who hid in the mountains and were never enrolled for a multitude of reasons, are now the ones excluded.

Ishi, the Last Yahi Yana

Some 200 tribes have become extinct. In 1911, a scraggly, raggedy Indian was discovered in Oroville, California foraging for food.

He had existed in the mountains for years as the sole survivor of the Yahi Yana tribe that still had approximately 2,000 members in 1848.

They named him Ishi which meant "man" in the Yana language. He died in 1916 in a California Museum.

Ishi the last Yana

The Last "Full-Blood" Kaw

The Kaw, formerly known as the mighty Kansa tribe, controlled some 20 million acres that stretched across Northern Kansas into Nebraska and Missouri. In April 2000, William Mehojah, the last full-blooded member of the Kaw tribe, died at 82. (Five years ago, there were four full-bloods.) Today, approximately 600 of 2,439 enrolled members live on 135 acres of trust land in Oklahoma and most tribal members have only a fraction of Kaw blood.

Mr. Mehojah at 82

Indian Languages

In 1492, approximately 500 Indian languages were spoken in North America. Some were linked by linguistic stocks, which meant that widely scattered tribal groups had some similarities in their languages.

Most of the 500 original languages of the Indian tribes are extinct. By 1995, 350 languages have become extinct and the remaining 150 are on the endangered list. Linguists predict that by 2020, 90 additional languages will be extinct, and by 2050, only 20 Indian languages will be spoken.

The U.N. Educational, Scientific and Cultural Organization says that languages need at least 100,000 speakers to pass from generation to generation.

Today, the Oneida and many other American Indian languages face extinction. Of an estimated 500 American Indian languages that existed when Columbus arrived in the New World, only 150 remain, according to the Indigenous Language Institute in Santa Fe.

Of these remaining 150 languages, 40 percent have nearly disappeared, with only a handful of tribal elders still speaking their respective languages. In North America, only 20 native languages, mostly from Southwest tribes, are still believed known to speakers in all living generations. Some projections suggest that by the year 2050, only these 20 languages will remain.

Wichita. Mandan. Osage. Shasta. The very languages that gave their names to the map of America are expected to disappear forever.

Among several Wisconsin Indian nations, the fate of the tribal language hangs on the lips of a few individuals.

"Our language is in a critical state right now," says Curt Summers, an Oneida language trainee in Oneida. "We have two elders that we work with on a daily basis, and 15 total fluent speakers out of a total of 15,000 registered Oneida."

Other state tribes fare better. The Indigenous Language Institute estimates 39 speakers still speak fluent Menominee. And Willard Lonetree, division manager of the Ho-Chunk language division in Mauston, estimates that about 400 Ho-Chunk still speak their native tongue in a tribe numbering more than 6,000.

More than half the 100 to 200 American Indian languages once spoken nationwide have only one or two fluent speakers left, according to retired University of Oregon linguistics professor Noel Rude. In Oregon, 19 of the 21 original languages are extinct.

Marie Smith, 83, of Anchorage, Alaska, says she's the last speaker of Eyak, a claim verified by linguists. She doesn't like the distinction. "It's horrible to be alone," Smith, who grew up in nearby Prince William Sound speaking Eyak, told the Associated Press in an interview. "I am the last person that talks in our language."

The language is the bedrock of any Indian tribe's culture, traditions and spirituality. The languages are dying out with the elders. Some parents are bilingual but their children and grandchildren are not interested in learning their Indian language for a variety of reasons.

In 1990, Congress passed the Indian Languages Act but essentially provided no funding for the program.

Indian Anthropologist

The experts have developed mathematical population models that can predict, within a percentage point or two, what will happen to tribes in the foreseeable future.

❖ "By the year 2050, only about 40% of the children born to CTUIR parents will be eligible for membership under the current enrollment ordinance." (Deward Walker's 1990 *A Study of Confederated Tribes of the Umatilla Indian Reservation Enrollment and Population.* Walker is a professor of Anthropology at the University of Colorado.)

❖ "These (Enrollment) policies, though replete with good intentions, may bring about the eventual extinction of Indian tribes." (Philip Zastrow's 1995 *Tribal Extinction: A Model for the Long-term Consequences of Tribal Enrollment Rules*. Zastrow is a professor at Humboldt State University and an enrolled member of the Hoopa Valley Tribe.)

❖ "As the idea of 'pan-Indianess' spreads, tribal identities are likely to blur. ...Indian people have high intermarriage rates, particularly with white people. In some ways, it's the only way the Indian population has been able to survive." (Russell Thornton Ph.D, professor of Anthropology at UCLA. Born and raised in Oklahoma and a member of the Cherokee Nation.)

Mitochondrial DNA Impact

In 10 or 20 years, a DNA analysis should be available for say, $28. I believe that most people who would take a DNA analysis, including Indians, would be very surprised by the results. When you consider the fact that Indians have been inter-tribally mixing for thousands of years and mixing inter-racially for 500 years, who can say unequivocally, that they know their definitive tribal blood composition? There is already a cadre of DNA companies already in place and knocking on the tribal doors.

This DNA scenario could be used against the Indians, if their claims are based on their tribal affiliation and some members do not meet the tribe's blood quantum requirements in the strictest sense.

The tribes use enrolled member numbers to get program money, but most services are not extended to the Indians once they leave the reservations. The scarcity of funds pits tribes against their urban counterparts.

Think about what Indians looked like 100 years ago and then try to imagine what Indians will look like 100 years from today. The face of Indians looked quite different 100 years ago than it does today, and they will look quite different 100 years from today.

CHAPTER 2 — TRIBES

Originally, an Indian tribe was a body of people bound together by blood ties who were socially, politically, and religiously organized, who lived together in a defined territory and who spoke a common language or dialect.

Indian tribes formed as part of a natural process that evolved over thousands of years. Indian tribal lifestyles and the limitations of the environment determined the number of people that could live in a given area. Indian tribe's social and political differences were important factors in the development of splinter clans, bands and tribes.

Each tribal history is a unique chapter in Indian History 101. Social scientists offer the premise that there may be other migration theories. For the purpose of our discussion, we will assume the prevalent theory that the Indian tribal pyramid began as hunters who crossed the Bering Straits in Alaska and began their migration over two continents.

The composition of today's tribes has been tremendously impacted by the federal government's relocation programs and the reservation system. Multiple tribes were relocated on common reservations and some tribes were split and relocated to several different reservations.

Federally-recognized Tribes

The United States government's legal definition for Indian tribes:

"Any Indian tribe, band, nation, rancheria, pueblo, colony or community which is recognized by the United States government as eligible for programs and services provided by the Secretary of the Interior to Indians because of their status as Indians."

❖ There are 563 federally-recognized tribes in the United States.

❖ 228 of those tribes are in Alaska.

❖ The spectrum ranges from several California tribal bands that have two or three members to the Cherokees of Oklahoma with 281,000 members and the Navajo Nation with 269,000 members. These two tribes represent 25% of the total Indian population.

❖ Approximately 200 tribes are extinct.

❖ The 1954 Termination & Relocation Act terminated 109 tribes.

❖ 245 tribes are in various stages of petition for federal recognition. (These tribes range in size from small bands to the Lumbees of North Carolina with over 40,000 members.)

❖ More than 46 tribes are state-recognized.

Petitioning Tribes

Petitioning for federal recognition is a long, expensive and ambiguous process. Most tribes do not have the resources to sustain a petitioning process that requires indeterminate years of tenacious perseverance.

There are seven basic requirements for federal tribal recognition:

1. Historical documentation of Indian ancestry.
2. Proof of political influence over members.
3. A list of all tribal members.
4. Proof that members do not belong to another tribe.
5. A copy of the tribal governing document.
6. The presence of a distinct tribal community.
7. The tribe must not be barred from a legal relationship with the United States government.

Since 1978, 245 groups have submitted their petition for acknowledgment through the administrative process:

❖ Approximately 72 have submitted completed petitions.
❖ To date, 41 of these completed petitioners have been finally resolved.
❖ The current work load consists of 15 under active consideration.
❖ 11 ready for active consideration.
❖ 2 decisions are in litigation.
❖ 4 are in post-final decision appeal process before the Interior Board of Indian Appeals.

Each year, one or two tribes manage to navigate the arduous process and receive recognition. The Lumbees of North Carolina have been petitioning for more than 100 years. The Little Shell Tribe of Chippewas of Montana were finally recognized in May, 2000, after petitioning for 108 years.

Tribal Sovereignty

Each Indian tribe considers itself a sovereign nation. Many tribes have recently decided that the politically correct reference will be "nations" rather than tribes. The issue of sovereignty has been a subject of long-running debate between the United States government and the tribes. The United States government negotiated treaties with the tribes as sovereign nations and promised certain inalienable rights and entitlements in exchange for land cessions.

By definition, sovereignty is supreme and complete political independence and self-government. A sovereign nation must have the ability to defend its borders, exercise authority over its citizens, and conduct its business free from outside interference.

Tribal sovereignty is a paradox because the United States government, while recognizing the tribes as domestic sovereign nations, has perpetuated a relationship of tribal dependence on the government.

Does Potter Valley Rancheria in California at three acres and one Indian have the same sovereignty as the Navajo Nation some 17 million acres and 269,000 people? The smaller tribes need to find refuge under the protective umbrella created by the larger stronger tribes.

The Interior Department has recently caused concern in the Indian community by its definition of "historic" tribes as those that have existed since time immemorial, whose powers derive from their un-extinguished, inherent sovereignty.

"Non-historic" tribes are those created under the 1934 Indian Reorganization Act that have only powers incidental to owning property and conducting business. Another division.

Yesterday's Promise — Today's Challenge

The following is an excerpt from the 1998 American Indian Research & Policy Institute:

> Challenges to the legal tenets of tribal sovereignty are not entirely new, but they are of increasing intensity. With the fervor of media attention focused on Indian gaming and the potential wealth it represents, many interest groups have formed and are embarking on new tactics to promote an anti-Indian sentiment. Perceptions by these interest groups about Indian policy, such as hunting and fishing rights negotiated in treaties, are misconstrued into statements of "rights" granted to a "special" population (Indians) that are not afforded to all citizens. These misperceptions about the true legal and political status of American Indians fuel the fire to use the courts as a problem solver.
>
> In addition, there is increased interaction between tribes and state governments that has a similar "chipping away" effect on the trust relationship between tribes and the United States Congress. This increased interaction follows years of disinterest on the part of state and local governments about the tribal people living on reservations; a disinterest that extended to American Indians living in urban areas as well. An example of the intensified relationships between tribal governments and state and local governments is the recent emphasis on taxing tribal governments for roads leading to and within Indian reservations or for funding other recreational activities, such as sports stadiums.
>
> The federal government is reducing or attempting to eliminate its trust relationship with American Indian

tribes through the devolution of social and economic support guaranteed to tribes. For example, the most recent welfare reform policies will cause tribes to deal with the state governments to access and acquire welfare benefits and other forms of social services for tribal members that were once funded under authority of the federal government. This pressure to forge relationships between tribes and state governments has the potential to critically alter the historical, legal, and sovereign relationship between tribes and the federal government both presently and in the future.

Challenges facing tribal governments from both internal and external forces remain a constant struggle for Indian leaders. In many ways, these challenges have changed little over time. Struggles over how tribes should be governed and by whom have been present since the inception of the Indian Reorganization Act of 1934. External pressures to reduce reservation land or to forfeit hunting and fishing rights have been a constant threat from state and local governments and non-Indian citizens.

These attacks on tribes and tribal sovereignty are propelled forward and are becoming increasingly more subtle. These threats seem to rely on the changing nature of internal tribal relations and tribal members' relationships to their reservations. Tribal leaders must return to or continue to utilize the strong foundation of traditional ways for governing their tribes. At the same time, tribal leaders and tribal members must possess an understanding of these current challenges, driven both internally and externally, and how these actions pose a tremendous threat to tribal sovereignty and American Indian tribes of the future.

Tribes Names

Generally speaking, today's tribal names are the result of mangled pronunciations or hybrid designations by early trappers and settlers. Several tribes have recently changed their official names to reflect tribal languages: the Papago to Tohono O'Odham, Winnebago to Ho-Chunk, Devil's Lake Sioux to Spirit Lake Nation, etc.

Jack D. Forbes, a professor at the University of California in Davis, California, published the *Atlas of Indian History*. An interesting feature of the study is a list of tribal names in their respective Indian language referenced to the English version of the same name.

Tribal Governments

Most tribal governments are organized democratically, that is, with an elected leadership. The governing body is generally referred to as a "council" and comprised of persons elected by vote of the eligible adult tribal members. The presiding official is the "chairman," although some tribes use other titles such as "principal chief," "president" or "governor." An elected tribal council, recognized as such by the Secretary of the Interior, has authority to speak and act for the tribe and to represent it in negotiations with federal, state, and local governments.

Tribal governments generally define conditions of membership, regulate domestic relations of members, prescribe rules of inheritance for reservation property not in trust status, levy taxes, regulate property under tribal jurisdiction, control conduct of members by tribal ordinances and administer justice.

Many tribes are organized under the Indian Reorganization Act (IRA) of 1934, including a number of Alaska Indian villages, which adopted formal governing documents (Constitutions) under the provisions of a 1936 amendment to the IRA. The passage in 1971 of the Alaska Indian Claims Settlement Act, however, provided for the creation of village and regional corporations under state law to manage the money and lands granted by the Act.

The Oklahoma Indian Welfare Act of 1936 provided for the organization of Indian tribes within the State of Oklahoma. Some tribes do not operate under any of these acts, but are nevertheless organized under documents approved of governments. Prior to reorganization, the tribes maintained their own, often highly developed, systems of self- government.

CHAPTER 3 — RESERVATIONS

Federally Recognized Reservations

The United States government's legal definition of an Indian reservation:

> **"An Indian reservation is an area of land held in trust by the federal government, reserved for Indian use."**

The Secretary of the Interior is the trustee for the United States. The Bureau of Indian Affairs (BIA) is responsible to the trustee for administration and management of Indian trust lands.

❖ There are 314 federally-recognized reservations, totaling some 56 million acres.

❖ Approximately 45 million acres are tribal trust lands.

❖ Approximately 11 million acres are allotted lands.

❖ There are approximately 43 state-recognized reservations.

❖ Indian reservations range in size from the one acre Sheep Ranch Rancheria in California to the Navajo Nation with some 17 million acres. A few reservations are nearly 100% tribal trust lands and others are almost entirely privately owned lands.

Reservation Resources

It is poetic justice that some of the once-desolate reservations have become valuable land due to minerals resources, pristine resources and urban locations.

Some Indian tribes have an impressive array of resources on their reservation trust lands.

- ❖ 40% of United States uranium deposits.
- ❖ 30% of western coal reserves.
- ❖ 4% of United States oil and gas reserves.
- ❖ 44 million acres in range and grazing.
- ❖ 5.3 million acres of commercial forest.
- ❖ 2.5 million acres of crop area.

Historically, Indians are allowed to occupy lands until there is a greater need for the "common good" usually based on economic avarice. The acquisitions were mandated by the Congressional political process.

- ❖ The Indian Removal Act of 1830 usurped the cultivated lands of the five "Civilized Tribes" in the Southeastern states.
- ❖ The 1874 discovery of gold in the Black Hills of South Dakota.
- ❖ Oklahoma Indian reservations (once known as "Indian Country") were dissolved after the discovery of oil during the 2–3 years prior to statehood in 1907.
- ❖ The Dawes Allotment Act of 1887 extracted some 90 million acres from Indian reservations.

When 1% of the United States population has use and control of a disproportionate amount of resources that the other 99% need or want, that 1% had better be a "tight" minority and able to defend their position, especially, if the 99% have depleted their resources. The 1% will need to be educated, economically solvent and have political clout to defend their turf.

More recently, the budget cuts and control of Indian gaming issues are examples of control and manipulation by Congressional politics. The 120-year history of negotiations between Indian tribes versus the United States government speaks for itself.

Congress giveth and Congress can taketh away.

The "Trail of Tears"

The Indian Removal Act of 1830 precipitated the infamous "Trail of Tears" that refers to the 1838 forced march of some 15,000 Cherokees from their coveted farmlands in the Southeastern United States to Oklahoma Indian territory. More than 4,000 Indians died during the march from disease, exposure and starvation.

In a broader context, the Trail of Tears was typical of the forced removal of some 60,000 members of the five "Civilized Tribes" (Cherokee, Chickasaw, Choctaw, Creek and Seminole) that lasted for nearly 10 years.

The forced removal was in violation of a Supreme Court decision by Chief Justice John Marshall in favor of the Indians, and President Andrew Jackson's infamous response: "John Marshall has made his decision, now let him enforce it."

The Dawes Allotment Act

On February 8, 1887, Congress enacted the General Allotment Act (GAA). This Act directed the division of tribal lands and "allotment" of them to individual Indians. The purpose was to accelerate the "civilization" of Indians by making them private landowners, successful farmers, and ultimately to assimilate them into society at large. By the 1930s it was widely accepted that GAA had, for the

Indian Land for Sale, 1910 (National Archives)

most part, failed.

Congressman Henry Dawes, author of the act, once expressed his faith in the civilizing power of private property with the claim that to be civilized was to "wear civilized clothes, cultivate the ground, live in houses, ride in Studebaker wagons, send children to school, drink whiskey and own property."

The Dawes Act or General Allotment Act of 1887
(Source: United States Statutes at Large 24:388–91)

CHAP. 119.—An act to provide for the allotment of lands in severalty to Indians on the various reservations, and to extend the protection of the laws of the United States and the Territories over the Indians, and for other purposes.

Be it enacted by the Senate and House of Representatives of the United States of America in Congress assembled, That in all cases where any tribe or band of Indians has been, or shall hereafter be, located upon any reservation created for their use, either by treaty stipulation or by virtue of an act of Congress or executive order setting apart the same for their use, the President of the United States be, and he hereby is, authorized, whenever in his opinion any reservation or any part thereof of such Indians is advantageous for agricultural and grazing purposes, to cause said reservation, or any part thereof, to be surveyed, or resurveyed if necessary, and to allot the lands in said reservation in severalty to any Indian located thereon in quantities as follows:

To each head of a family, one-quarter of a section;

To each single person over eighteen years of age, one-eighth of a section;

To each orphan child under eighteen years of age,

one-eighth of a section; and

To each other single person under eighteen years now living, or who may be born prior to the date of the order of the President directing an allotment of the lands embraced in any reservation, one-sixteenth of a section: Provided, That in case there is not sufficient land in any of said reservations to allot lands to each individual of the classes above named in quantities as above provided, the lands embraced in such reservation or reservations shall be allotted to each individual of each of said classes pro rata in accordance with the provisions of this act: And provided further, That where the treaty or act of Congress setting apart such reservation provides the allotment of lands in severalty in quantities in excess of those herein provided, the President, in making allotments upon such reservation, shall allot the lands to each individual Indian belonging thereon in quantity as specified in such treaty or act: And provided further, That when the lands allotted are only valuable for grazing purposes, an additional allotment of such grazng lands, in quantities as above provided, shall be made to each individual.

SEC. 2. That all allotments set apart under the provisions of this act shall be selected by the Indians, heads of families selecting for their minor children, and the agents shall select for each orphan child, and in such manner as to embrace the improvements of the Indians making the selection. where the improvements of two or more Indians have been made on the same legal subdivision of land, unless they shall otherwise agree, a provisional line may be run dividing said lands between them, and the amount to which each is entitled shall be equalized in the assignment of the remainder of the land to which they are entitled under his act: Provided, That if any one entitled to an allotment shall fail to make a selection vithin four years after the President shall lirect that allotments may be made on a particular reservation, the Secretary of the Interior may direct the agent of such tribe or band, if such there be, and if there be no agent, then a special agent appointed for that purpose, to make a selection for such Indian, which selection shall be allotted as in cases where selections are made by the Indians, and patents shall issue in like manner.

SEC. 3. That the allotments provided for in this act shall be made by special agents appointed by the President for such purpose, and the agents in charge of the respective reservations on which the allotments are directed to be made, under such rules and regulations as the Secretary of the Interior may from time to time prescribe, and shall be certified by such agents to the Commissioner of Indian Affairs, in duplicate, one copy to be retained in the Indian Office and the other to be transmitted to the Secretary of the Interior for his action, and to be deposited in the General Land Office.

SEC. 4. That where any Indian not residing upon a reservation, or for whose tribe no reservation has been provided by treaty, act of Congress, or executive order, shall make settlement upon any surveyed or unsurveyed lands of the United States not otherwise appropriated, he or she shall be entitled, upon application to the local land-office for the district in which the lands arc located, to have the same allotted to him or her, and to his or her children, in quantities and manner as provided in this act for Indians residing upon reservations; and when such settlement is made upon unsurveyed lands, the grant to such Indians shall be adjusted upon the survey of the lands so as to conform thereto; and patents shall be issued to them for such lands in the manner and with the restrictions as herein provided. And the fees to which the officers of such local land-office would have been entitled had such lands been entered under the general laws for the disposition of the public lands shall be paid to them, from any moneys in the Treasury of the United States not otherwise appropriated, upon a statement of an account in their behalf for such fees by the Commissioner of the General Land Office, and a certification of such account to the Secretary of the Treasury by the Secretary of the Interior.

SEC. 5. That upon the approval of the allotments provided for in this act by the Secretary of the Interior, he shall cause patents to issue therefor in the name of the allottees, which patents shall be of the legal effect, and declare that the United States does and will hold the land thus allotted, for the period of twenty-five years, in trust for the sole use and benefit of the Indian to whom such allotment shall have been made, or, in case of his decease, of his heirs according to the laws of the State or Territory where such land is located, and that at the expiration of said period the United States will convey the same by patent to said Indian, or his heirs as aforesaid, in fee, discharged of said trust and free of all charge or incumbrance whatsoever: Provided, That the President of the United States may in any case in his discretion extend the period. And if any conveyance shall be made of the lands set apart and allotted as herein provided, or any contract made touching the same, before

the expiration of the time above mentioned, such conveyance or contract shall be absolutely null and void:
Provided, That the law of descent and partition in force
in the State or Territory where such lands are situate shall
apply thereto after patents therefor have been executed
and delivered, except as herein otherwise provided; and
the laws of the State of Kansas regulating the descent and
partition of real estate shall, so far as practicable, apply to
all lands in the Indian Territory which may be allotted
in severalty under the provisions of this act: And provided further, That at any time after lands have been
allotted to all the Indians of any tribe as herein provided,
or sooner if in the opinion of the President it shall be for
the best interests of said tribe, it shall be lawful for the
Secretary of the Interior to negotiate with such Indian
tribe for the purchase and release by said tribe, in con-
formity with the treaty or statute under which such reservation is held, of such portions of its reservation not allotted as such tribe shall, from time to time, consent to sell,
on such terms and conditions as shall be considered just
and equitable between the United States and said tribe
of Indians, which purchase shall not be complete until
ratified by Congress, and the form and manner of exe-
cuting such release prescribed by Congress: Provided
however, That all lands adapted to agriculture, with or
without irrigation so sold or released to the United States
by any Indian tribe shall be held by the United States for
the sale purpose of securing homes to actual settlers and
shall be disposed of by the United States to actual and
bona fide settlers only tracts not exceding one hundred
and sixty acres to any one person, on such terms as Congress shall prescribe, subject to grants which Congress

may make in aid of education: And provided further, That no patents shall issue therefore except to the person so taking the same as and homestead, or his heirs, and after the expiration of five years occupancy therof as such homestead; and any conveyance of said lands taken as a homestead, or any contract touching the same, or lieu thereon, created prior to the date of such patent, shall be null and void. And the sums agreed to be paid by the United States as purchase money for any portion of any such reservation shall be held in the Treasury of the United States for the sole use of the tribe or tribes Indians; to whom such reservations belonged; and the same, with interest thereon at three per cent per annum, shall be at all times subject to appropriation by Congress for the education and civilization of such tribe or tribes of Inians or the members thereof. The patents aforesaid shall be recorded in the General Land Office, and afterward delivered, free of charge, to the allottee entitled thereto. And if any religious society or other organization is now occupying any of the public lands to which this act is applicable, for religious or educationl work among the Indians, the Secretary of the Interior is hereby authorized to confirm such occupation to such society or organization, in quantity not exceeding one hundred and sixty acres in any one tract, so long as the same shall be so occupied, on such terms as he shall deem just; but nothing herein contained shall change or alter any claim of such society for religious or educational purposes heretofore granted by law. And hereafter in the employment of Indian police, or any other employes in the public service among any of the Indian tribes or bands affected by this act, and where Indians can perform the duties required, those Indians who have availed themselves of the provisions of this act and become citizens of the United States shall be preferred.

SEC. 6. That upon the completion ef said allotments and the patenting of the lands to said allottees, each and every nmmber of the respective bands or tribes of Indians to whom allotments have been made shall have the benefit of and be subject to the laws, both civil and criminal, of the State or Territory in which they may reside; and no Territory shall pass or enforce any law denying any such Indian within its jurisdiction the equal protection of the law. And every Indian born within the territorial limits of the United States to whom allotments shall have been made under the provisions of this act, or under any law or treaty, and every Indian born within the territorial limits of the United States who has voluntarily taken up, within said limits, his residence separate and apart from any tribe of Indians therein, and has adopted the habits of civilized life, is hereby declared to be a citizen of the United States, and is entitled to all the rights, privileges, and immunities of such citizens, whether said Indian has been or not, by birth or otherwise, a member of any tribe of Indians within the territorial limits of the United States without in any manner affecting the right of any such Indian to tribal or other property.

SEC. 7. That in cases where the use of water for irrigation is necessary to render the lands within any Indian reservation available for agricultural purposes, the Secretary of the Interior be, and he is hereby, authorized to prescribe such rules and regulations as he may deem necessary to secure a just and equal distribution thereof among the Indians residing upon any such reservation;

and no oother appropriation or grant of water by any riparian proprietor shall permitted to the damage of any other riparian proprietor.

SEC. 8. That the provisions of this act shall not extend to the territory occupied by the Cherokees, Creeks, Choctaws, Chickasaws, Seminoles, and Osage, Miamies and Peorias, and Sacs and Foxes, in the Indian Territory, nor to any of the reservations of the Seneca Nation of New York Indians in the State of New York, nor to that strip of territory in the State of Nebraska adjoining the Sioux Nation on the south added by executive order.

SEC. 9. That for the purpose of making the surveys and resurveys mentioned in section two of this act, there be, and hereby is, appropriated, out of any moneys in the Treasury not otherwise appropriated, the sum of one hundred thousand dollars, to be repaid proportionately out of the proceeds of the sales of such land as may be acquired from the Indians under the provisions of this act.

SEC. 10. That nothing in this act contained shall be so canstrued to affect the right and power of Congress to grant the right of way through any lands granted to an Indian, or a tribe of Indians, for railroads or other highways, or telegraph lines, for the public use, or condemn such lands to public uses, upon making just compensation.

SEC. 11. That nothing in this act shall be so construed as to prevent the removal of the Southern Ute Indians from their present reservation in Southwestern Colorado to a new reservation by and with consent of a majority of the adult male members of said tribe.

Approved, February 8, 1887.

Impact of Allotment

What is mixed or checkerboard land ownership and how did it happen? Mixed land ownership describes the pattern of land ownership often resembling a checkerboard that exists on many reservations. Title to the land is held by different entities including the tribe, Indian individuals, the state, the county, the federal government and non-Indian groups or individuals.

When tribes signed treaties they gave up millions of acres of aboriginal territory for designated reservation areas. Why are these treaty lands now owned by non-Indian entities, creating mixed land ownership on many reservations? For most tribes, mixed land ownership began with the Dawes Act better known as the Allotment Act passed in 1887. Prior to the passage of this Act, all lands within the boundaries of the reservation were owned by tribes as stipulated in their respective treaties or executive orders.

Outside interests, such as timber, railroad companies, and homesteaders, wanted more Indian land and sought to gain use and control of select lands within reservation treaty boundaries. These entities put pressure on the federal government to allow access and title to these lands.

In total disregard of the treaties, the Dawes Act was implemented. Individual tribal members were allotted 160, 80, and 40-acre parcels. Remaining reservation (treaty) lands were declared surplus and sold to non-Indians through surplus land sales.

The Allotment Act was one of the most devastating pieces of legislation ever passed in terms of reduction of tribally owned lands, breakdown of Indian tribal culture, and creation of some of the greatest bureaucratic barriers to Indians use and control of the land base. This action was in direct violation of the treaty agreements. Prior to the Allotment Act tribal land holdings totaled 138 million acres. By the end of the allotment period in 1934, nearly 90 million acres held passed out of Indian tribal ownership.

Today, there are approximately 11 million acres of allotted lands on 150 reservations affecting some 300,000 allottees.

The Indian Land Working Group

In 1991, the 1st Annual Indian Land Consolidation Symposium was held in Pendleton, Oregon, and was co-sponsored by the Confederated Tribes of the Umatilla Reservation (CTUIR), the First Nations Development Institute, and the Northwest Renewable Resources Center. The CTUIR had recently embarked on their new Nations Project whereby the tribes were seeking to restore their original treaty homeland, and to address issues related to their allotted lands. They thought the best way to do this would be to network with other tribes in similar situations and consequently organized the First Indian Land Symposium.

The Indian Land Working Group (ILWG) was an outgrowth of this first symposium, where attendees decided that the tribes and Indian individuals should continue to share their knowledge and ideas on how to address problems stemming from mixed (Indian and non-Indian) land ownership of Indian homelands. The more than 150 conference attendees moved to form the ILWG, which today continues to conduct the annual symposiums.

In addition to the symposium, the ILWG: conducts workshops and meetings related to land issues throughout the year; has produced an Indian Land Consolidation Manual; developed a draft legislative proposal which addresses land issues related to estate planning, data development, real estate transactions, acquisition financing, and Indian probate; and has produced a series of educational videos which seek to empower tribes and Indian landowners by sharing strategies related to recovery, consolidation, use and preservation of allotted homelands.

Who Lives on Reservations?

Today, most reservations have non-Indian residents and landowners living within the boundaries of reservations.

- ❖ 11 million acres (20%) within reservation boundaries are owned by non-Indians.
- ❖ Nearly one-half (46%) of the reservation population are non-Indians.

CHAPTER 4 — THE BUREAU OF INDIAN AFFAIRS (BIA)

BIA Acknowledgement

Most of the material is this chapter has been paraphrased from the Bureau of Indian Affairs (BIA) and other sources.

The BIA is not the enemy. In fairness to the BIA today, it should be understood that, in 176 years, many past sins and much of the chaos was institutionalized and inherited. I personally know and have worked with BIA personnel over the years who are capable and dedicated.

In order to address divisive issues and be fair, it is prudent to state the BIA position and purpose in its own words.

Mission Statement

The Bureau of Indian Affairs' mission is to enhance the quality of life, to promote economic opportunity, and to carry out the responsibility to protect and improve the trust assets of American Indians, Indian tribes and Alaska Indians. We will accomplish this through the delivery of quality services, and maintaining government-to-government relationships within the spirit of Indian self-determination.

Vision Statement

The Bureau of Indian Affairs is a challenging and dynamic place to work. We provide high quality services in a timely and professional manner. We have the organizational flexibility to meet the changing needs of our customers. Our employees are committed, knowledgeable and empowered. Our polices are clear, consistent and supported throughout the organization. We manage for excellence, fostering cooperation and coordination in consultation with Indian Tribes while supporting self-determination and tribal sovereignty.

A Short History

While the Bureau of Indian Affairs did not receive congressional authorization until 1834, ten years after it had been administratively established by the Secretary of War, the stage was set for its creation in the earliest days of the United States government. One of the first actions taken by the Continental Congress in 1775 was to name a Committee on Indian Affairs. The committee established three departments of Indian Affairs and called upon such prominent Americans as Benjamin Franklin and Patrick Henry to assume leadership roles in the operation of these offices.

Henry Knox, Secretary of War, assumed responsibility for Indian affairs with the ordinance of August 7, 1786. The first Congress continued administration of Indian affairs within the War Department, established in 1789, with direction to the Secretary to place armed militia at the disposal of Indian commissioners "for negotiating treaties with the Indians."

Trading houses were maintained from 1786 to 1822 to supply Indians with necessary goods and, in exchange, to offer them a fair price for their furs. This was a matter of importance and concern for the government. As a result, the office of Superintendent of Trade was created in 1806 to place some controls on the practice of trading with Indians.

Without authorization from Congress, Secretary of War John C. Calhoun on March 11, 1824, created what he called the Bureau of Indian Affairs. The logical choice to head this office was Thomas McKenny, who had been Superintendent of Trade when that post was abolished two years earlier.

The matter of giving its approval to the establishment of an Indian office was vigorously debated in the Congress, but before such a measure passed, the lawmakers created the position of Commissioner of Indian Affairs.

On July 9, 1832, Congress authorized the President "to appoint by and with the advice and consent of the Senate, a Commissioner of Indian Affairs, who shall, under the direction of the Secretary of War, and agreeable to such regulations as the President may, from time to time, prescribe, have the direction and management of all Indian affairs, and of all matters arising out of Indian relations."

The first President-appointed Commissioner was Elbert Herring. His salary was set at $3,000 per year.

In the first session of the 23rd Congress in 1834, the Committee on Indian Affairs of the House of Representatives produced three bills dealing with Indian affairs. These included measures to (1) organize a Department of Indian Affairs, (2) regulate trade with Indians, and (3) provide for the establishment of a western territory in which the Indians should be separated.

The third measure did not pass, but the other two were enacted into law. On June 30, 1834, the Bureau of Indian Affairs came into being through what has since become known as the organic law of the Indian office.

The organizational structure of Indian affairs during the 1800s primarily included two types of field jurisdictions, superintendents and agents. The superintendents were generally responsible for Indian affairs within a geographical area, usually a territory. Agents, some reporting to superintendents and others directly to the Indian affairs office, were concerned with the affairs of one or more tribes.

The Bureau of Indian Affairs was to remain in the War Department for 15 years after its creation by Congress. An act on March 3, 1849, established the Home Department of the Interior and Indian affairs passed from military to civilian control.

Development of the reservation system gained momentum in the mid-1850s after experimentation with the reservation policy in California. The role of the Bureau changed in the last quarter of the 1800s and specialized activities such as irrigation, forestry, Indian employment, law enforcement, health and construction became increasingly more important.

Education of young Indians came to the forefront in 1879, when the first off-reservation boarding school was established at Carlisle, Pennsylvania. Chemwa Indian School in Oregon, Haskell Institute in Kansas, and Chilocco Indian School in Oklahoma were opened within the next five years. Other schools were to follow.

After World War II, a system of area offices was established and area directors were made responsible for administering all Indian programs within their geographical locations. This three-tier structure continues today, with organizational lines extending from Washington, DC to the area offices to the agencies at the reservation level.

Until 1973, the Bureau of Indian Affairs was placed organizationally under an Interior Department assistant secretary whose principle responsibilities revolved around land and water resources or other Interior programs. Indian affairs was a secondary concern of this official and frequently Indian goals and objectives were opposed by other Interior agencies.

This situation was partially corrected when Morris Thompson became commissioner in 1973 and reported directly to the Secretary of the Interior.

Finally, in 1977, the post of Assistant Secretary of Indian Affairs was created, thereby assuring the Bureau of a voice in policy matters within the Interior Department. Forrest Gerard, a member of the Blackfeet Indian tribe, became the first to fill this office.

Trust Responsibility

The following is an excerpt from the American Indian Policy & Research Institute.

The progress that the tribes made in the last 50 years is rolling back to the 1950s where people are talking about terminating Indian tribes. "The conscience of the dominant society has changed," said Bobby Whitefeather, Red Lake tribal chairman, in opening discussion of the relationship between the federal government and Indian tribes.

The United States Constitution, which is patterned after the Great Law of the Iroquois Confederacy, recognized Indian tribes as sovereign nations. During the colonial period and the infancy of the United States, tribes exerted great influence on the Europeans living in North America. Tribes were considered military and political equals, and were often key allies in power struggles between the colonies and the Old World countries.

However, when the military power of Indian nations waned, some people in the United States began to view Indians as subservient, even though the legal nation to nation relationship remained the same.

As late as the 1830s, the Supreme Court recognized that the relationship between Indian tribes and the United States was that of one nation to another. This relationship did not involve states or local governments. In fact, in *Worchester v. Georgia,* the Supreme Court ruled that because of the nationhood of the Cherokee Tribe, the laws of Georgia could have no force on them.

"The words 'treaty' and 'nation' are words of our own language, selected in our diplomatic and legislative proceedings, by ourselves, having each a definite and well understood meaning. We have applied them to Indians, as we have applied them to the other nations of the earth. They are applied to all in the same sense," writes the Supreme Court.

What has changed in the twentieth century is not the legal relationship between United States and Indian tribes, but rather the perspective. As the United States followed Manifest Destiny westward consuming land and resources, tribes began to be looked upon as dependent domestic nations instead of as foreign nations. As domestic nations within another nation, the federal government has a responsibility to protect the interests of Indians.

"The trust relationship evolved judicially and survived occasional congressional attempts to terminate the government's obligations to Indians. In theory, the trust relationship exists to protect tribes and individual Indians. However, in practice, the federal trustee has at times not worked in the best interests of the intended beneficiaries," according to attorney Larry Leventhal, writing for the Hamline Law Review. "One way to conceptualize trust responsibility is to think of it as treaty responsibility," said Dennis King, an Oglala tribal council member. The federal government still has the responsibility to honor agreements and treaties, which is why it is important for Indians to be knowledgeable about the treaties that affect them.

Often the promises made by the United States in treaties are enforceable under the trust doctrine. In a 1983 decision, *United States v. Mitchell,* the Supreme Court developed a standard for determining liability arising from a breach of trust responsibility.

It's important to note that although federal trust responsibility arises out of the nationhood of tribes, the trust doctrine also applies to individual Indians. This is unlike sovereignty and sovereign immunity, which can only be applied to nations.

The American Indian Policy Review Commission (AIPRC), established by Congress in 1975, called federal trust responsibility the most important as well as the most misunderstood concept in federal government-Indian relations.

Part of the misunderstanding may stem from actions of Congress. The federal government has often acted inconsistently with and in opposition to the principles of trust doctrine, leaving the public and many tribes confused.

The AIPRC defined the United States as a fiduciary whose actions were to be judged by the highest standards. Because the federal government has so much control over the resources of Indian nations and individual Indians, the trust doctrine is implied in dealings even if not implicitly stated.

Trust responsibility affects everything the federal government is involved in, from education and health care to trust lands and the Bureau of Indian Affairs.

During his term in office, President Bill Clinton acknowledged the broad trust responsibility of the federal government. In an Executive Memorandum, he directed all cabinet heads and departments to work with tribes in a government-to-government relationship.

Trust responsibility has come under challenge by Congress as budget cuts have reduced services guaranteed to tribes through treaties. "When things are not going well, the federal government wants out from under trust responsibility," Whitefeather said.

Public attention has focused on a small number of tribes that have been visibly successful through casino gambling. Public perception tends to lump all tribes into that same category. Clearly there is a need for more public awareness of the legal and political framework that has shaped federal-tribal relations.

Many Indians have been re-examining trust responsibility too, and finding that the federal government has not lived up to its principles. In just one example, the Bureau of Indian Affairs mismanagement and complete lack of accounting of funds has resulted in the disappearance of $2.4 billion dollars of Indian money.

BIA Indian Programs Budget

For Immediate Release: February 3, 2003
Contact: Nedra Darling
(202) 219-4152

Trust Reform and Economic Development
See Funding Increases
Under BIA FY2004 Budget Request
*Additional funding sought for trust improvements
and tribal economies.*

WASHINGTON, D.C. — President Bush has proposed a $2.31 billion budget for the Bureau of Indian Affairs (BIA) for Fiscal Year 2004, an increase of $62.0 million over the FY 2003 request, to improve the Interior Department's management of individual Indian and tribal trust assets, to operate new tribally-operated detention centers and to develop tribal economies. The request also maintains the President's commitment to eliminate the school maintenance backlog and provide tribes with greater opportunities to directly operate BIA schools. Payments for Indian water and land claims settlements also continue.

"With this budget request, the President makes clear his firm commitment to improving the lives of Indian people through trust reform, education and economic development," said acting Assistant Secretary — Indian Affairs Aurene M. Martin. "The Bureau will be prepared to meet these goals with Congress' support."

The FY2004 budget request provides new funding to support the Department's plan to reform management of its fiduciary obligations to the Federally recognized tribes and individual Indians. The request includes increases of $32.0 million to modernize information technology systems and security to support trust and non-trust programs; $13.0 million to expand a pilot program to reduce the fractionalization of individual Indian land ownership interests into a nationwide effort and $7.6 million for enhanced resource management programs related to trust assets.

The BIA oversees a 185-school system comprised of elementary and secondary day and boarding schools serving almost 48,000 students. The FY2004 budget request for school construction and repair is $292.6 million, including $131.4 million to replace at least seven BIA-funded schools including Enemy Swim Day School, Waubay, S.D.; Isleta Elementary School, Isleta, N.M.; Mescalero Apache School, Mescalero, N.M.; Navajo Preparatory School, Farmington, N.M.; Pueblo Pintado Community School, Cuba, N.M.; Turtle Mountain High School, Belcourt, N.D., and Wingate High School, Ft. Wingate, N.M.

Under the Bureau's FY2004 $528.5 million school operations budget request, an increase of $3.0 million in administrative cost grants is sought to encourage more tribes to exercise their authority to operate BIA-funded schools by providing full funding for start-up costs for the first year of tribal operation of a BIA school. In the School Year 2001–2002, the BIA directly operated one-third of elementary and secondary schools, including four of seven off-reservation boarding schools. The remaining two-thirds of the schools are operated by tribes under BIA contract or grant.

To enhance economic development in Indian Country, the FY2004 budget request seeks $1.0 million in increased funding to expand the BIA's Indian Loan Guaranty Program to assist tribes with financing for business operations. The increased funding will leverage $20 million in additional guaranteed and insured loans.

To meet Federal requirements for authorized settlements resolving long-standing tribal claims in New Mexico and Oklahoma, the FY2004 budget request includes funding increases to complete the Santo Domingo Pueblo settlement ($6.7 million) and for the first payment on the recent Cherokee, Choctaw and Chickasaw settlement ($10.0 million). The budget also maintains funding at current levels for five additional settlements and reflects decreases due to the completion of two settlements.

Furthermore, funding is requested to continue support for the BIA's Law Enforcement Program to improve public safety and justice in Indian Country. The FY2004 budget request seeks an increase of $10.0 million for the operation of new detention centers.

BIA continues to make progress in the President's management agenda for improving management and performance of the Federal government by practicing the Secretary's vision for citizen-centered management excellence. The FY2004 budget for BIA supports the Department's outcome goals to fulfill Indian trust responsibilities and advance quality communities for Tribes. BIA has worked extensively to integrate the budget with the performance goals in the Department's new unified strategic plan.

The School Operations, School Construction and Indian Land Consolidation programs were assessed using the Administration's Program Assessment Rating Tool (PART). The PART process identified actions needed to clarify program purpose and design, and provided recommendations to improve strategic planning, program management and program results. BIA has begun to work on improvements recommended as a result of the assessment.

The Assistant Secretary — Indian Affairs has responsibility for fulfilling the Department's trust responsibility to American Indian and Alaska Native tribes and individuals, as well as promoting tribal self-determination, education and economic development. The Assistant Secretary also oversees the BIA, which is responsible for providing services to approximately 1.5 million American Indians and Alaska Natives from the nation's 563 federally-recognized tribes.

BIA: Friend or Foe?

Indian issues are mired in a morass of demographics complicated by convoluted tribalism:

❖ Nearly 2.5 million self-declared Indians.
❖ Approximately 1.7 million enrolled tribal members.
❖ 563 federally-recognized tribes.
❖ 150 different languages and dialects.
❖ 314 federally-recognized reservations.
❖ 46 state-recognized reservations.

The monumental task of administration and management of this demographic nightmare is the responsibility of the Bureau of Indian Affairs. During its 176 year history, the BIA has often been the subject of severe criticism in the execution of its responsibilities on behalf of American Indians.

The BIA and Indians are diametrically opposed philosophically. The BIA has the trust responsibility to ensure that tribes receive their lawful treaty entitlements in the form of special programs; and on the other hand and at the same time encourage self-determination and independence as domestic sovereign nations.

It's a "Catch 22." On one hand, the BIA is the pipeline for federal programs and on the other hand it interferes and exerts too much government control over sovereign tribal affairs. Is it time for BIA reform or should the BIA be phased out and true tribal sovereignty exercised? (Is "dependent sovereign" an oxymoron?)

The BIA has been and still is a tremendous resource for Indians. The BIA website: *www.doi.gov/bureau-indian-affairs.html* is a great resource when it is available.

The BIA website as well as the BIA mail servers are temporarily unavailable due to the Cobell Litigation. Please continue to check from time to time. We have no estimate on when authorization will be given to reactivate these sites.

CHAPTER 5 — THE INDIAN CONDITION

Third World conditions are still the reality for most of Indian America and they are still the poorest race of people in the country with regard to health, education and welfare. The prosperity of a handful of hugely successful gaming tribes has eclipsed the grinding poverty of the vast majority of Indians.

Health

The Indian Health Service (IHS) is the principal federal health care provider and health advocate for American Indian/Alaska Native people, and its goal is to raise their health status to the highest possible level. The IHS currently provides health services to approximately 1.4 million American Indians and Alaska Indians who belong to more that 563 federally-recognized tribes in 34 states.

The majority of Indian people served by IHS live on or near reservations in some of the most remote and poverty stricken areas of the country where other sources of health care are less available. For many, the IHS is the only source of care. Urban Indian health programs provide limited services to more than 150,000 Indians living in 34 states.

The IHS is organized as 12 area offices which are located throughout the United States. Within the 12 regions are 550 health care delivery facilities, including 49 hospitals, 214 health centers, and 280 health stations, satellite clinics, and Alaska village clinics operated by the IHS and tribes.

The system delivers comprehensive personal and public health services including over 80,000 hospital admissions and almost 7 million ambulatory medical care visits per year. In addition, dental services, nutrition, community health, sanitation facilities (water supply and waste disposal), injury prevention and institutional environmental services are provided.

❖ The IHS has over 14,500 employees.

❖ The IHS annual appropriation is approximately $2.8 billion.

The following statistics are from the Regional Differences in Indian Health 1998–1999: Extrapolated by the Indian Health Service/Office of the Director/Public Affairs Staff September 2002.

❖ Alcohol mortality is 770% greater than for all other races combined.

❖ Fetal Alcohol Syndrome (FAS) is 33 times higher than other Americans.

❖ Tuberculosis is 750% greater than all other Americans.

❖ Diabetes is 6.8 times greater than all other Americans.

❖ Pneumonia and influenza is 61% greater than all other Americans.

❖ Homicide is 210% greater than all other Americans.

❖ Accidental deaths are 280% higher than all other Americans.

❖ Suicides are 190% higher than all other Americans.

❖ One in six adolescents has attempted suicide which is 4 times more often than all other teenagers.

Education

"Education is your most powerful weapon. With education you are the white mans equal; without education you are his victim, and so shall remain all your lives. Study, learn, help one another always. Remember there is only poverty and misery in idleness and dreams but in work there is self respect and independence."
— Chief Plenty Coups, *Crow Tribe*

Office of Indian Education Programs (OIEP) has responsibility for 185 elementary and secondary schools and dormitories as well as 27 colleges. OIEP colleges, schools and dormitories are located on 63 reservations located in 23 states serving approximately 60,000 students representing 238 different tribes.

One can visualize this wide-geographic spread by watching the sun rise on the Passamaquoddy Reservation, the first stream of daylight to touch the United States on the east cost of Maine and then watching the sun set on the Quileute Reservation, the last stream of daylight to touch the United States on the west coast of Washington.

The majority of the schools are located in Arizona and New Mexico, with most of these schools located on the Navajo Reservation, but also including the Pueblos and Apache of New Mexico and the Pima, Tohono O'odham, Hopi and Apache of Arizona. The area with the second greatest number of schools encompasses the states of North Dakota and South Dakota on the reservations of the Sioux Nation, Mandan, Hidatsa, Arikara and Ojibwe. The area with the third greatest number of schools is located in the northwest region of the United States.

The remaining schools are scattered on reservations throughout the United States from the Seminole and Miccosukee in the Everglades of southern Florida to the Choctaw in Mississippi and Cherokee in North Carolina; from the Saulte Ste. Marie Chippewa and Potowatomi in the Upper Peninsula of Michigan to the Sac and Fox of Iowa and the Kickapoo of Kansas; from the Saboba in southern California to Muckleshoot near Puget Sound in Washington.

At present more than half of the schools are operated through grants to tribes and local school boards.

The lack of Internet access is a major concern for the BIA school system.

Student performance and participation is far below the national average:

❖ 52% finish high school.
❖ 17% attend college.
❖ 4% graduate from college.
❖ 2% attend graduate school.

Why Indian People Are At Risk

*Our schools have failed to nurture the intellectual devel-
opment and academic performance of many Indian children, as is evident from their high dropout rates and negative attitudes toward school.*

*Our schools have discouraged the use of Indian lan-
guages in the classroom, thereby contributing to a weak-
ening of the Indians' resolve to retain and continue the
development of their original languages and cultures.*

*Indian lands and resources are constantly besieged by
outside forces interested in further reducing their original
holdings.*

*Political relationships between the tribes and the federal
government fluctuate with the will of this United States
Congress and decisions by the courts.*
— Excerpt from the United States Dept. of Education
"Indian Nations At Risk Task Force," 1991

Economic Disparity

Indians are disadvantaged in the development of business acumen as entrepreneurs. The disparity between the income of Indians and mainstream economics is widening in direct proportion to
their lack of experience, opportunity and resources. From a historical perspective, Indians are recent arrivals to the political and economic arena.

❖ 75% of the work force earn less than $7,000 per year.
❖ 45% live below the poverty level.
❖ The average unemployment rate is 45%.
❖ Unemployment on some reservations is 90%.
❖ Most housing is inadequate and substandard. For instance, Navajos, who have the largest reservation and tribe with the most resources, endure the following conditions:

  ○ 46% have no electricity.
  ○ 54% have no indoor plumbing.
  ○ 82% live without a telephone.

These Third World living conditions are typical of most reservation communities. Poor health care, miserable poverty and substandard education are a daily fact of life for most Indians.

"During 1992, we will honor this country's Indian people as vital participants in the history of the United States. This year gives us the opportunity to recognize the special place that Indians hold in our society, to affirm the right of Indian tribes to exist as sovereign entities and to seek greater mutual understanding and trust."
— President George H. W. Bush,
March 1992

"Indian Tribes should be subject to state law. My view is that state law reigns supreme when it comes to the Indians, whether it be gambling or any other issue,"
— Gov. George W. Bush (R-TX)
Presidential candidate, 1999

Indians have made sporadic uprisings that receive brief notoriety and media exposure. However, as public and political attention wanes, it is business as usual. An objective evaluation of the

Indian condition would conclude that systems and programs employed for the last 100 years are not working very well.

The most effective strategy to incapacitate and destroy any organization is by internal dissention. Indians are particularly vulnerable to this strategy because of egocentric tribalism. They have been divided historically by circumstance and design.

Reality Check

The United States is outraged at oppression and abuse of indigenous people in other countries, while at home, Indians are a dispossessed and disenfranchised people in their own homeland. The hypocrisy should be an embarrassment to the country that is considered the world leader of democracy and guardian of human rights. It is incumbent upon the United States government to set an example for the world with regard to treatment of the indigenous Indian people of this country.

Almost everyone agrees that Indians have legitimate grievances that have not been equitably resolved, however, most Indian issues are obscured by current national and international crises.

To establish a realistic perspective, let's list some of the country's major domestic and world problems. Rank them in your order of priority:

According to the Census Bureau: 20 million people have died from AIDS since the epidemic began two decades ago. 40 million people now live with HIV, the virus that leads to AIDS, and barring major medical breakthroughs most of these people are expected to die within the next 10 years. That's 11,000 people dying per day = 456 people dying per hour.

❖ According to United Nations officials, 11 million Third World children, most of them babies, die each year of preventable causes. That's 30,137 children dying per day = 1,256 children dying per hour.

- ❖ War in Iraq and Afghanistan.
- ❖ Nuclear weapons threat of North Korea, Iran, etc.
- ❖ Homeless people.
- ❖ Drug problems.
- ❖ Education.
- ❖ Health care.
- ❖ Social Security.
- ❖ Space programs.
- ❖ Environmental pollution.

The list is endless and everybody has an agenda. Now rank American Indian issues on this list.

Congress is the political and economic power base of the country and Congress is motivated by a combination of politics, economics, public opinion and lobbied interests. There are few Indian advocates in Congress.

As Senator DeConcini of Arizona so aptly stated from a Congressional perspective, "Nobody gives a damn about Indians."

Although major Indian civilizations had flourished centuries before the white man's arrival, Indian cultures were not recognized by Europeans as established civilizations. Nor have they been given the appropriate recognition for their significant contributions to the development of this country.

Indian issues are emotionally charged and logic is often clouded by the heat of the moment. It is very difficult to be objective. Attitude and the law are often a matter of convenience and purpose as the United States government justifies its treatment of Indians.

The dilemma is compounded by social complacency and misinformation. Negative stereotyping continues and serves as an effective conduit for discrimination and prejudice that lead to exploitation. Neither attitudes nor morality can be legislated; they can be reformed only by education and time.

Adaptability is fundamental to most Indian problems. Indians are polarized between tradition and culture on one hand and adaptation to the progress of the dominant culture on the other. The issue seems to be the appropriate degree of adaptability.

Obviously, a lesser degree of adaptability is required from a Navajo sheepherder or an artist living a traditional lifestyle on the reservation than from a Navajo attorney or a business person living in the Phoenix metro area.

Even traditional Reservation Indians have adapted to one degree or another. Horses, guns and clothing were early adaptations. Modern home construction, electricity, running water, automobiles, television and phones are evidence of more recent adaptation.

Being Indian is not just a matter of blood quantum, it is a state of being and a spirituality. Traditionally, Indian spirituality is an integral part of daily living in harmony with the rhythms of nature.

Historically, most Indian tribes were primarily a migratory people. The migrations were dictated by the laws of nature and more recently, by the mandates of the dominant society. A cultural consequence of these migrations is an attachment of spiritual significance to geographic features.

Each Urban Indian must determine what degree of adaptation is required to function as a productive member of society and yet preserve his or her Indian connections. Some Indians wear long hair, braids, jewelry and apparel as a declaration, while others use some or none of the trappings.

Nothing is forever and the only thing for sure is change. Indians are a very small minority (less than 1% of the United States population) who are a step behind mainstream society by all socio-economic standards. They are clinging to a past-life that may be morally and ecologically correct. However, change is the natural order of things and life moves on.

CHAPTER 6 — FREQUENTLY ASKED QUESTIONS (FAQS)

The following are some of the most commonly asked questions about American Indians. Some of the answers are partially paraphrased from old BIA documents.

Are Indians United States Citizens?

As ludicrous as it may sound, Indians were categorically granted United States citizenship by the 1924 Indian Citizenship Act. Citizenship had been conferred upon approximately two-thirds of the Indian population through treaty agreements, statutes, naturalization proceedings, and by service in the Armed Forces with an honorable discharge in World War I.

With citizenship came all rights and obligations of any other United States citizen. Theoretically, enrolled tribal members have dual citizenship.

Do Indians Serve in the Armed Forces?

Yes. Indians have the same obligations for military service as other United States citizens. They have fought in all American wars since the Revolution.

In the Civil War, they served on both sides. Eli S. Parker, Seneca from New York, was at Appomattox as aide to General Ulysses S. Grant when General Robet E. Lee surrendered, and the unit of Confederate Brigadier General Stand Watie (Cherokee) was the last to surrender.

During World War I, Indians demonstrated patriotism (6,000 of the more than 8,000 who served were volunteers) and moved Congress to pass the Indian Citizenship Act of 1924.

During World War II, 25,000 Indian men and women, mainly enlisted Army personnel, fought on all fronts in Europe and Asia, winning (according to an incomplete count) 71 Air Medals, 51 Silver Stars, 47 Bronze Stars, 34 Distinguished Flying Crosses, and two Congressional Medals of Honor. The most famous Indian exploit of

World War II was the use by Navajo Marines of their language as a battlefield code, the only such code that the enemy could not break.

In the Korean conflict, there was one Indian Congressional Medal of Honor winner.

During the Vietnam War, 41,500 Indians served in the military forces.

In 1990, prior to Operation Desert Storm, some 24,000 Indian men and women were in the military.

Approximately 3,000 served in the Persian Gulf with three among those killed in action.

One out of every four Indian males is a military veteran and approximately 50 percent of tribal leaders today are military veterans.

Are Treaties Still Made with Indian Tribes?

No. The first treaty was made with the Delawares in 1778 and in 1871 Congress declared that no Indian nation would be recognized for the purpose of making treaties. Since then, relations with Indian groups are by Congressional Acts, Executive Orders, and Executive Agreements. Between 1778 and 1871, the United States Senate ratified 370 Indian treaties. At least 45 others were negotiated with tribes but were never ratified by the Senate.

Originals of all the treaties are maintained by the National Archives and Records Service of the General Services Administration. A duplicate of a treaty is available upon request for a fee. The agency will also answer questions about specific Indian treaties. Write to: Diplomatic Branch, National Archives and Records Services, Washington, DC 20408

Do Indians Pay Taxes?

Yes. They pay the same taxes as other citizens with the following exceptions:

Federal income taxes are not levied on income from trust lands held for them by the United States;

State income taxes are not paid on income earned on an Indian reservation;

State sales taxes are not paid by Indians on transactions made on an Indian reservation;

Local property taxes are not paid on reservation or trust land.

What are Tribal Treaty Entitlements?

Any special rights that Indian tribes or members of those tribes have are generally based on treaties or other agreements between the United States and tribes. Indian tribes paid a heavy price to retain certain "sovereign" rights and entitlements by relinquishing much of their land to the United States.

The inherent rights they did not relinquish are protected by United States law. Among those may be hunting and fishing rights and access to religious sites.

Do Indians Get Monthly Government Checks?

No individual is automatically paid for being an Indian. The federal government may pay a tribe or an individual in compensation for damages for losses resulting from treaty violations, for encroachments on Indian lands, or for other past or present wrongs.

A tribe or an individual may also receive a government check for payment of income from their lands and resources. This occurs because their resources are held in trust by the Secretary of the Interior and payment for their use has been collected from users by the Federal Government on their behalf. Fees collected from oil or grazing leases are an example of this situation.

Some 47 tribes that have successful casinos pay "per capita" checks to members after social programs are funded and tribal infrastructures have been built.

Do Indians Get a Free College Education?

No. An individual does not automatically receive funding because of Indian ancestry. The Indian higher education program provides financial aid to eligible students, based on demonstrated financial need, who have plans to attend an accredited institution of higher education.

A student must obtain an application packet and other financial aid information from their tribe, BIA or Area Office of Indian Education Programs. The Higher Education Grant Program is available to an individual who is a member of a federally-recognized Indian tribe.

Some tribes that have successful casinos offer to provide a college education for tribal members.

Do Indian Tribes Have Their Own Governments?

Most do. The governing body of the tribe is generally referred to as the tribal council and is made up of council members elected by vote of the adult members of the tribe and presided over by the tribal chair person. The tribal council elected in this way has authority to speak and act for the tribe and to represent it in negotiations with federal, state and local governments.

Tribal governments, in general, define conditions of tribal membership, regulate domestic relations of members, prescribe rules of inheritance for reservation property not in trust status, levy taxes, regulate property under tribal jurisdiction, control conduct of members by tribal ordinances and administer justice.

Many tribes are organized under the Indian Reorganization Act (IRA) of 1934, including a number of Alaska Native villages, which adopted formal governing documents under the provisions of a 1936 amendment to the IRA. However, the passage of the Alaska Native Claims Settlement Act of 1971 has provided for the creation of village and regional corporations under state law for the purpose of managing the money and lands granted by that act. The Oklahoma Indian Welfare Act of 1936 provides for the organization of Indians tribes within the State of Oklahoma. Some tribes do not operate under any of these acts but are organized under documents approved by the Secretary of the Interior. Some tribes continue their traditional form of government.

Do All Tribes Have Reservations?

There are 563 federally-recognized tribes and 314 federally-recognized reservations. Obviously, a significant number of federally-recognized tribes do not have federally-recognized reservations.

There are 228 federally-recognized tribes in Alaska and 37 in Oklahoma. There is one federally-recognized reservation in Alaska (Annette Island) and one in Oklahoma (Osage).

The destiny of American Indians is at a crossroads. American Indians must prepare to take control of their destiny, as gently as possible. The next battles will be won by attorneys whose weapons are the legal briefs and laptop computers. The skirmishes will be fought in courtrooms and political battles waged in Congressional committees.

Section 3:
The Future

It seems a basic requirement to study the history of our Indian people. America has much to learn about the heritage of our American Indians. Only through this study can we as a nation do what must be done if our treatment of the American Indian is not to be marked down for all time as a national disgrace."

— President John F. Kennedy, 1963

It is incumbent upon the Indian people to shoulder their share of responsibility for conduct that has contributed to their negative image. It is the responsibility of the Indian community to replace that negative image with a more accurate and positive image.

Indians had two important characteristics in days of old:

❖ They were natural athletes. Before the horse, Indian people traveled by foot. They were great long-distance runners and superb hunters. The diet was natural and lean. Today, frybread is an Indian staple — white flour dropped into sizzling lard and sometimes sprinkled with sugar.

❖ They were great storytellers and eloquent orators. A few tribes had written languages but most did not, although some tribes developed pictographs and petroglyphs.

Indian tribes have contributed immensely to the plagiarism of certain culture, traditions and ceremonies by public display at pow wows. The public is invited and coyly asked not to take pictures of certain sacred ceremonies. Perhaps there should be public pow wows and private pow wows, each with its own agenda and purpose.

Can we realistically expect today's society to be compassionate about Indian peoples problems? Today's society is oblivious to memories of the Great Depression, World War I and World War II, has only fading memories of Vietnam and Civil Rights marches of the 1960s and is unconcerned about atrocities perpetrated generations before they were born.

Today's generation will not assume the sins of their forefathers.

Changing of the Guard

Public empathy toward American Indian issues will diminish with each succeeding generation. *Today's generation will not assume the sins of their forefathers.* Too much time has passed and there are too many contemporary issues that have a higher priority.

American Indian destiny is at a crossroads. Indians must prepare to take control of their destiny, as gently as possible. The next battles will be won by attorneys whose weapons are the legal briefs and laptop computers. The skirmishes will be fought in courtrooms and political battles waged in Congressional committees.

Historically, when political and economic forces covet American Indian land and resources, social conscience is compromised.

"The fault dear Brutus, lies not in our stars but within ourselves."

— William Shakespeare, *Julius Caesar*

CHAPTER 1 — STRATEGIC PLANNING

Tribal Self-Determination

Indians are survivors. They have survived 400 years of genocide and 100 years of BIA dominance and government control. They have a strong spirituality closely tied to the land, and their religions reflect a respect for the mysterious powers of nature. For the moment, it appears that the pendulum of social conscience has swung in favor of the Indians. People of conscience are empathetic to the plight of Indians. In the academic community there are concerted efforts to include a more accurate account of Indian history and culture.

Empathy is wonderful but the time has come for Indians to take control of their own destiny. Historically, when political and economic forces covet Indian land and resources, social conscience is compromised. Avarice has the inherent ability to justify and rationalize its actions. The ends justify the means. The goals can now be accomplished through clever paper and political manipulations, rather than the overt physical aggressions of the past.

The idea that Indian people can live in tranquil harmony with nature on reservations is a dangerous illusion. Today's Indians cannot walk the path of their ancestors. The last bargaining chip is the reservations and their respective resources. Indians must take appropriate precautions to protect those remaining resources.

For thousands of years, tribalism was an instinct that was necessary for survival. Tribalism has an up side and a down side. The up side is that tribalism is a source of Indian strength, culture and tradition. The down side is that tribalism has always been at the heart of Indian dissension.

Egocentric tribalism is not conducive to the development of significant national political or economic power. Democracy is a game of numbers and the majority rules.

- ❖ Of the 2.5 million self-declared Indians in the country, approximately 1.7 million are enrolled. The total Indian population is less than 1% of the total population of 281 million.
- ❖ Nearly all reservation lands are held in "trust" by the United States government. The Congressional fox is guarding the Indian chicken coop.
- ❖ 11 million acres (20%) within reservation boundaries are owned by non-Indians.
- ❖ Nearly one-half (46%) of the reservation population are non-Indians.
- ❖ Less than 10% of contemporary Indians speak their Indian language.

Indians continue to be a political embarrassment and an economic thorn in the side of federal and state governments.

There are literally hundreds of programs, agencies, organizations and publications that are concerned with Indian issues. The effective entities must develop a centralized communication system that nurtures interaction and networking. The internet is a window of opportunity for Indians to make a quantum leap in networking and communication.

Indians can no longer rely on the "big brother" paternalistic benevolence of the United States government. Government subsidies for necessities of life are not the answer to Indian future. The answers are education, political unity and economic independence.

80% of all reservation lands are held in "trust" by the US government. The Congressional fox is guarding the American Indian chicken coop.

CHAPTER 2 — POLITICS

"Two years ago I made an unscheduled visit to the town of Guadalupe, Arizona, home to 5,600 people of Hispanic and Yaqui Indian descent. The Third World conditions there, unpaved roads, dilapidated housing, high unemployment, made an indelible impression on me. I vowed to do all in my power to bring hope and opportunity to Guadalupe and other economic disaster areas like it across America."

— Jack Kemp, Secretary of Housing and
Urban Development, July 1992

> ### America's conscience has been appeased with regard to the American Indian condition by misinformation, disinformation and complacency

As tribal and organization attorneys use the legal system to enforce entitlements, reparations and tribal sovereignty, an Indian political Armageddon is looming on the horizon. It's not a matter of if, it's a matter of when. At some point in the foreseeable future, the political issue will be the national interest versus Indian interest.

When the United States Congress decides that it is in the best interest of the nation to confiscate the mineral resources and/or to implement the "highest and best use" of land reserved exclusively for the use of a small minority, it will happen.

In a democracy, when the interest of a 99 percent majority is in direct conflict with a 1 percent minority, the majority will prevail. At less than 1 percent of the population, Indians will have to be a "tight" minority, politically and economically, in order to survive.

If necessary, clever lawyers will declare the treaties unconstitutional for one reason or another. There will be impassioned debates with a wailing and gnashing of teeth by Indian tribes based on what is right, what is just and what is fair. But when the dust settles, a Congressional committee (most of whom are totally ignorant about Indian America) will vote and the organized majority will prevail.

As anti-Indian forces mount and organize, Indians continue to bicker, squabble and quarrel among themselves, to the extent that they cannot present a united front within their own tribes, to say nothing of organizing 563 different tribes as a united voice. Civil disobedience is an option, but not a very good one. If Indian America does not have a politically organized and well-funded defense strategy, they will lose.

Congress, the BIA and the anti-Indian establishment view this type of greedy, avaricious and inane behavior with great delight and further evidence that Indians are incapable of handling their own affairs.

Do Tribes Have Political Clout?

Ben Nighthorse Campbell (R-CO) is the only Indian in Congress and he is retiring this year. Indians do not have collective political clout. They must deal with the fact that a divided people are a vulnerable and manageable people. Remember Senator DeConcini's comment: "Nobody gives a damn about Indians."

For the first time in history, gaming tribes have the resources and are beginning to flex their political muscle by political contributions to candidates who are advocates for their agenda.

In many states (South Dakota, North Dakota, Washington, California, Arizona, and New Mexico) where the Indian population is concentrated, the Indian vote can be the crucial swing vote in close races.

In the South Dakota 2000 election, Democratic Sen. Tim Johnson trailed Republican Rep. John Thune by about 700 votes the morning after the election. Johnson won by 528 votes after ballots from the Pine Ridge Reservation were counted.

Voter-fraud charges followed both the state and Bennett County results. A *Wall Street Journal* editorial blasted Tim Johnson as "the Oglala Sioux's senator" and said the Democrats "stole" the election.

War may be too strong a word, but the American Indian people and their lands are essentially under siege. They are in a battle for survival.

American Indian voters played a similar role in Washington State in the 2000 election when they helped oust United States Senator Slade Gorton, seen as openly hostile to Indian interests, and helped elect Maria Cantwell by a narrow margin.

Can Indians Vote?

Indians have the same right to vote as other United States citizens.

❖ In 1948, the Arizona Supreme Court declared the disenfranchising interpretation, that declared Indians as incompetent, as unconstitutional of the state constitution and allowed Indian people to vote.
❖ In 1953, a Utah state law stated that persons living on Indian tribal reservations were not residents of the State and could not vote, was repealed.
❖ In 1954, Indian tribes in Maine who were not federally-recognized, at the time, were given the right to vote.
❖ In 1962, New Mexico extended the right to vote to Indian people.

Do Indians Vote?

Indians are notorious for their lack of participation in the political process. Estimates are as low as 10% voter turnout in past elections. Most Indians feel that the political process is a white man's game, and they traditionally do not participate.

War may be too strong a word, but the Indian people and their lands are essentially under siege. They are in a battle for survival. It's a different kind of cold war that's insidious by nature and nurtured by apathy. In order for Indians to survive, they must view each election as a battle.

Each Indian vote is an arrow. Each time a Indian doesn't vote, it's the same as a vote for the opposition. If Indians do not participate in the decision making political process by voting, other interest groups, with their own agendas, will make those decisions for them.

Politicians respond to votes. If an important Indian issue is presented to the Congressional Committee on Indian Affairs, and the Chair of the Committee opens his door on a Monday morning to find 10,000 Indian people faxes or emails it would have a tremendous impact on the decision-making process. And it is possible.

As of January 1, 1996, most United States citizens can register to vote by mail. A new national voter-registration form has been designed to make it more convenient for Americans to register for the first time or to make a change of address, name or political party.

Citizens can request the form from their state election officials, usually by phone, and use it to register to vote in all but five states: Arkansas, Virginia, New Hampshire (where it will only be accepted as a mail-in registration form for absentee voters), North Dakota (which does not require voters to register), and Wyoming, that will not permit the form's use.

Indians are not the only non-voters. In an embarrassing example to the world's other democracies, only 38.7% of all United States citizens of voting age bothered to exercise their right and responsibility in the 2000 election.

In 1994, the Navajo tribal election and the general election were on the same day and polling places were side by side. This made it easy for Navajo voters to choose their state and federal representatives.

Voter registration should be a requirement for enrollment. The Saginaw Chippewa's require voter registration for tribal voting and elections. They could both be done at the same time.

In those areas that have a large Indian population, particularly in the West, Indian groups are finding that they have the power to influence the outcome of major elections. Indian voters are beginning to flex their political muscle.

Voter registration should be a requirement for enrollment.

121

Have Indians Held Public Office?

United States Senate:

❖ Hiram R. Revels, Lumbee from Mississippi, 1870–1871

❖ Mathew Stanley Quay, Abenaki or Delaware from Pennsylvania, 1887–1899 and 1901–1904

❖ Charles Curtis, Kaw from Kansas, 1907–1912 and 1915–1929 (Vice-President from 1929–1933)

❖ Robert L. Owens, Cherokee from Oklahoma, 1907–1925

❖ Ben Nighthorse Campbell — Current Republican Senator from Colorado

United States House of Representatives:

❖ Charles Curtis, Kaw from Kansas, 1893–1907

❖ Charles D. Carter, Choctaw from Oklahoma, 1907–1927

❖ W. W. Hastings, Cherokee from Oklahoma, 1915–1921 and 1923–1935

❖ Will Rogers, Jr., Cherokee from California, 1943–1944

❖ William G. Stigler, Chocktaw from Oklahoma, 1944–1952

❖ Benjamin Reifel, Rosebud Sioux from South Dakota, 1961–1971

❖ Clem Rogers McSpadden, Cherokee from Oklahoma, 1972–1975

Indians also served in and now hold office in a number of state legislatures. Others currently hold or have held elected or appointive positions in state judiciary systems and in county and city governments, including local school boards. Larry Echo Hawk, an enrolled member of the Pawnee Tribe, served as attorney general of Idaho from 1992 to 1994.

CHAPTER 3 — PUBLIC RELATIONS

Indians have never had and still don't have control of their public image or identity. The most aggravating circumstance is when the people perpetuating cultural slander say they do not see anything wrong with it and have the unmitigated ignorant gall to say they feel they are "honoring" the Indians. Shouldn't the Indians have something to say about that?

What's Wrong With "Squaw" As a Name for Indian Women?

Trappers, settlers and frontiersmen consorted with Indian women and often took Indian wives. The social attitude toward this practice was reflected by the term "squaw" and "squawman" with reference to Indian women and their European male counterparts. Within the context of the times, the designation "squaw" and "squawman" may have had various connotations, but the derogatory meaning was always clear.

Over the attrition of time, the term "squaw" was commonly used as a generic reference to Indian women, until it was recently revealed that "squaw" was an Algonquin word for female genitalia.

The issue became a point of contention in the Indian community and especially with Indian women. So please do not make the mistake of calling an Indian woman a squaw.

What's Wrong with "Redskins" as an NFL Team?

The Washington "Redskins" would not survive a season as the Washington "Blackskins" or "Yellowskins" or "Brownskins." For some games, a pig is painted red, a simulated Indian tribal chief's warbonnet is strapped to the pig's head and it's run around the field to incite fan frenzy. I wonder how the black players on the team and the fans would feel if the pig were painted black with an Afro wig strapped on its head and run around the field?

Within the context of the times, the designation "squaw" and "squawman" may have had various connotations, but the derogatory meaning was always clear.

The infamous "tomahawk chop" and chanting is another example of mindless and thoughtless racism. These images are repeatedly broadcast over national television in living color. I can still see Ted Turner and Jane Fonda at a "Redskins" football game gleefully doing the "tomahawk chop." These are people who supposedly hold liberal political views and are concerned with social equality issues.

Would the Cleveland Indians "Wahoo" cartoon mascot survive a season as the Cleveland "Kikes" or the Cleveland "Chinks" or the Cleveland "Sambos" or the Cleveland "Wops"?

It is demeaning and racist to use cartoon caricatures and cultural symbolism of a race of people as professional or academic, sports team mascots. There are names and mascots that are not offensive and damaging to any race of people.

I'm sure that it was not the intent of most sports fans to be malicious or racist. However, the hurt and racism inflicted on Indian people, especially the young, is still the same, regardless of intent. It's similar to the definition of sexual harassment; the intent of the harasser is not important, it's the effect on the harrassee that matters. To be this mindless and thoughtless in today's society is immoral, inappropriate and unconscionable.

This is another example of the lack of Indian political clout. If it were a black mascot, the NAACP would impose a Washington Redskins boycott in a New York minute.

CHAPTER 4 — AMERICAN INDIAN BUSINESS

Do Indians Own Businesses?

According to the United States Census, the number of American Indian-owned companies grew by more than 80% during the 1990s. Indian businesses now number 197,300, employ 298,700 workers, and generate $34 billion in annual revenues.

Approximately 20,000 of those businesses are located on reservations. Indians are making the transition from supplier to entrepreneur as they prepare to make the quantum leap from the blanket to the boardroom.

Indian arts and crafts are a multi-million dollar business with domestic and global markets. The role of Indians in the marketplace has traditionally been as the supplier of arts and crafts products. Almost all Indian arts and crafts retail stores and businesses are owned by non-Indian people.

State and Regional Chambers of Commerce:

❖ Arizona American Indian Chamber of Commerce.
❖ Southern California American Indian Chamber of Commerce.
❖ Rocky Mountain Indian Chamber of Commerce.
❖ Northwest American Indian Chamber of Commerce.
❖ Texas American Indian Chamber of Commerce.
❖ Minnesota American Indian Chamber of Commerce.
❖ Oklahoma American Indian Chamber of Commerce.
❖ Wisconsin American Indian Chamber of Commerce

Indian Business Organizations.
❖ National Center for American Indian Enterprise Development.
❖ Indian Business Alliance.
❖ National Indian Business Association.
❖ Indian Business Connection.
❖ Arizona Indian Economic Coalition.
❖ Arizona American Indian Tourism Association.

Almost all Indian arts and crafts retail stores and businesses are owned by non-Indian people.

Casinos seem to be a quick-fix basis for cash flow — a short term solution for long-term problems.

Are Indian Tribes Getting Rich From Casinos?

Gaming is the current economic and political issue in Indian country. The issue of Indian sovereignty hangs in the balance as Indians cautiously negotiate the maze of overlapping state and federal jurisdictions and control.

Casinos seem to be a quick-fix basis for cash flow and a short-term solution for long-term problems. It is very difficult to argue with success but the jury is still out on the long-term ramifications of gaming on Indian social and economic development.

A handful of the Indian casinos, with smaller enrollments near large metro areas, are generating significant revenues and are distributing per capita payments. Theoretically and literally, some tribal members have become millionaires in a short period of time. Most tribal casinos generate more modest revenues.

This brings up a number of issues: Does this wealth translate into shared wealth with alienated or disconnected tribal members and their Urban Indian counterparts? What will be the attitude of the federal government and the public towards subsidy programs as the tribal coffers fill? Will health, education and entitlement subsidy programs continue for tribal members who are considered millionaires?

What will be the attitude and reaction of adjacent non-Indian communities toward the Indian gaming bonanza? Will there be a saturation of the gaming market with a casino on every corner? Or will there be a backlash if casino money machines absorb too much discretionary income and gambling becomes a blight on society?

As of this printing, California voters passed Proposition 5 which technically allows California's 107 federally-recognized tribes to open two casinos each. Some estimates indicate there could be as may as 113,000 slot machines in the state (there are about 130,000 slots in Las Vegas). It won't happen overnight, but California could eventually give Atlantic City and Las Vegas a run for their money. Sixty tribes have already signed gaming compacts.

After years of failed government programs, Indian reservations are among the poorest communities in the United States: The Shannon County Oglala Sioux Reservation in South Dakota is ranked lowest in the United States. Indian unemployment is six times the national average, and Indian health, education and income statistics are among the worst in the country.

Indian gaming is providing a means to self-sufficiency for tribal nations, and is also creating jobs and economic activity in local non-Indian communities and states where tribal gaming operations are located.

Who Regulates Indian Tribal Gaming?

Indian land is not governed by state law unless a federal law places it under state law. The Supreme Court held that even if a tribe is under state law, state gaming regulations do not apply on Indian trust land.

In 1988 Congress passed the Indian Gaming Regulatory Act. This law allows traditional Indian gaming as well as bingo, pull tabs, lotto, punch boards, tip jars and certain card games on tribal land. However, it requires a tribal/state compact for other forms of gaming such as cards or slot machines.

The National Indian Gaming Commission was established by Congress to develop regulations for Indian gaming. For more information contact the National Indian Gaming Commission, 9th Floor, 1441 L Street, NW, Washington, DC 20005, (202) 632-7003.

National Indian Gaming Association (NIGA)
224 Second Street SE
Washington, DC 20003
202-546-7711 Phone
202-546-1755 Fax

What will be the attitude of the federal government and the public towards subsidy programs as the tribal coffers fill?

NIGA Library and Resource Center Indian Gaming Facts

Size:

❖ Total number of federally-recognized Indian Tribes: 563

❖ Number of tribal governments engaged in gaming (Class II or Class III): 224

❖ Number of tribal governmental gaming operations: 354 (several Tribes operate more than one facility)

❖ Number of states with tribal governmental gaming: (Class II or Class III) 28

❖ Number of tribal-state gaming compacts: 249

Revenue:

❖ Tribal governmental gaming revenue in 2002: $14.5 billion (21% of total gaming industry)

❖ Many tribes operate gaming facilities primarily to generate employment

Employment:

❖ Total number of jobs: 400,000

❖ National percentage of Indian to non-Indian employees: 75% non-Indian, 25% Indian

❖ In areas of high unemployment like North and South Dakota, 80% of Tribal governmental gaming employees are Indian

Land:

❖ NIGA requires that land taken into trust status must:
  1. Benefit the Tribe
  2. NOT be detrimental to the surrounding community
  3. Be approved by the State Governor

❖ Only 23 total land-into-trust acquisitions since 1988 for gaming purposes

❖ Only three off-reservation land-into-trust acquisitions since 1988 (only 78 total acres)

Federal Recognition:

❖ Only 15 tribes have received Federal Recognition through the "Federal Acknowledgement Process" since 1978

❖ Only one of those tribes has gaming

❖ 16 petitions for recognition have been denied since 1978

Pathological Gambling:

❖ National prevalence rate of 0.8 percent for lifetime pathological gambling

❖ Compare lifetime figures for:
    Alcohol dependence — 13.8 percent
    Drug dependence — 6.2 percent
    Major depression — 6.4 percent

❖ Indian tribes have model programs for problem gamblers. In many areas, like Arizona, North Dakota and Connecticut, Indian Tribes are the primary funding source for such programs

Use Of Net Revenues:

❖ Revenues from Tribal Governmental gaming must be used in five specific areas. The Indian Gaming Regulatory Act (25 U.S.C. 2710 [Sec. 11]), states net revenues from any tribal gaming are not to be used for purposes other than to:

❖ Fund Tribal Government operations or programs

❖ Provide for the general welfare of the Indian tribe and its members

❖ Promote Tribal economic development

❖ Donate to charitable organizations

❖ Help fund operations of local government agencies

Who is and who isn't "American Indian" must be redefined by current criteria that will result in a rational and equitable solution.

Per Capita Payments:

❖ Three-fourths of gaming tribes devote all of their revenue to tribal governmental services, economic and community development, to neighboring communities and to charitable purposes and do not give out per capita payments

❖ Tribal government services, economic and community development, general tribal welfare, charitable donations and any requirements for aid to local governments must be provided for before a tribe can file for a "Revenue Allocation Plan."

❖ The Secretary of Interior must approve any per capita payments as part of a "Revenue Allocation Plan."

❖ Only about one-fourth of tribes engaged in gaming distribute per capita payments to tribal members (73 Tribes).

❖ Tribal members receiving per capita payments PAY FEDERAL INCOME TAX on these payments

Regulation:

❖ Tribal governmental gaming is regulated on three levels.

   1. Indian Nations are primary regulators of Indian gaming. Under the Indian Gaming Regulatory Act (IGRA), tribes establish the basic regulatory framework for Indian gaming.

   2. State regulation may be included in tribal/state compacts for Class III gaming.

   3. Federal agencies enforce laws relating to Indian gaming, including the National Indian Gaming Commission, the Interior Department, the Justice Department, FBI, IRS, Secret Service and the Treasury Department's Financial Crimes Enforcement Network

❖ Federal law makes it a crime punishable by up to ten years in prison to steal, cheat, or embezzle from an Indian gaming operation, and that law is enforced by the FBI 18 USC ss. 1163.

CHAPTER 5 — TEN YEAR AGENDAS

"Before we can set out on the road to success, we have to know where we are going, and before we can know that, we must determine where we have been in the past."
— John F. Kennedy, 1963

Indians are a small minority (1%) who have the unique feature of millennial ties to this land. They are survivors with a common bond who have withstood 400 years of "ations:" extermination, relocation, termination and assimilation. Indians are survivors. Through all the trials and tribulations, they have sustained a sense of humor. Indians have lost most battles, but not the war.

Immigrants, of all races, come to this country with a worn suitcase and a dream. Ten years later, many are educated and prosperous. Are Indians any less capable? Indians have the responsibility, to those ancestors who fired arrows against cannons and survived against overwhelming odds, to make that survival meaningful.

Indians have had time and opportunity to help correct the course of their own destiny. They must divorce themselves from the "helpless victim" mindset that blames the government for their station in life (even if it's true). The time has come for Indians to help themselves. All that life owes any of us is opportunity, and no one ever said that life was going to be fair.

Public empathy toward Indian issues will diminish with each succeeding generation. Today's generation will not, and probably should not, assume the sins of their forefathers. Too much time has passed and there are too many contemporary issues that have a higher priority.

Indians must prepare by education to take control of their destiny, as gently as possible. The next battles will be won by warriors in three-piece suits whose weapons are the briefcase and laptop computers. The skirmishes will be fought in courtrooms and battles won in Congressional committees.

But that brief period of recrimination is over because the nation's conscience has been appeased by the attrition of time.

> *The only thing for sure in this life is change, and adaptability is an absolute for the survival of a species or a civilization.*

Indian destiny is at a crossroads and the moment is at hand. Indians are a privileged people who want exclusivity. Indians are a special people, but they cannot be a separate people.

The only thing for sure in this life is change, and adaptability is an absolute for the survival of a species or a civilization. People lament for the "good old days," a time when life was simpler and basic values were solid. Sometime in the future, today will be someone's "good old days."

The Good Old Days...100 Years Ago

❖ Ninety percent of all United States physicians had no college education. Instead, they attended medical schools, many of which were condemned in the press and by the government as "substandard."

❖ More than 95 percent of all births in the United States took place at home.

❖ Some medical authorities warned that professional seamstresses were apt to become sexually aroused by the steady rhythm, hour after hour, of the sewing machine's foot pedals. They recommended slipping bromide — which was thought to diminish sexual desire — into the women's drinking water.

❖ Most women only washed their hair once a month and used borax or egg yolks for shampoo.

❖ Only 14 percent of the homes in the United States had a bathtub.

❖ Only 8 percent of the homes had a telephone.

❖ Marijuana, heroin, and morphine were all available over the counter at corner drugstores. According to one pharmacist, "Heroin clears the complexion, gives buoyancy to the mind, regulates the stomach, and is a perfect guardian of health."

- ❖ Coca-Cola contained cocaine instead of caffeine.
- ❖ Plutonium, insulin, and antibiotics hadn't been discovered yet. Computers, Scotch tape and canned beer hadn't been invented.
- ❖ The average wage in the United States was twenty-two cents an hour. The average United States worker made between $200 and $400 per year.
- ❖ Sugar cost four cents a pound. Eggs were fourteen cents a dozen. Coffee cost fifteen cents a pound.
- ❖ There were only 8,000 cars in the United States and only 144 miles of paved roads.
- ❖ The maximum speed limit in most cities was ten mph.
- ❖ Ten percent of United States adults couldn't read or write and only 6 percent of all Americans had graduated from high school.
- ❖ The population of Las Vegas, Nevada was thirty.
- ❖ There were only 230 reported murders in the United States annually.
- ❖ The average life expectancy in the United States was 47.

No one will argue against the importance of traditional values and lifestyles. But even traditions must evolve. I'm sure that what Indians consider traditional today is not the same as it was 500 years ago, 200 years ago or even 100 years ago. Most Indians had a seasonal migratory lifestyle and, in some cases, had to relocate because of droughts or other conditions beyond their control. When geography changes, so do traditions.

Times change. The younger generation of Indian women are not going to knead dough and cook frybread over an open fire outside the hogan. Nor are they going to sit cross-legged in front of a loom weaving a rug for 10 or 12 hours a day.

At less than 1% of the population, American Indians will have to be a "tight" minority, politically and economically, in order to survive.

Not all traditions, cultural or religious, were good. In the light of today's knowledge, some were funny, some were dumb, and some were barbaric and cruel.

The very best time of your life is right now. Not yesterday when life was simpler. Not tomorrow when life will be easier. We are part of the most exciting time in history with more opportunities than ever before. Of course there are problems, there always have been and there always will be.

We are all a work in progress. We are all a composite of each other. Life is a learning experience from crib to coffin. A process of evolution. If you do not have the ability to adapt to change, you will not survive the long haul. The trick is to keep what was good about the old traditions and blend them with new traditions.

Indians must develop an agenda that will result in a healing process for the country and all Indians. To meet the challenges of the future, Indians will need to develop a realistic three-tier, ten-year agenda to take control of their destiny:

Individual Agenda

❖ Education, education, education.

❖ The road from poverty to success is paved by education.

❖ Fiscal responsibility — Develop a save first mentality as opposed to a credit mentality. We are programmed from childhood into adolescence to be good credit risks so that the financial establishment will extend credit that we wouldn't need if we trained properly during these informative years. The first generation of parents will struggle with themselves and their children but after that it will begin to take effect fiscally. Indian people will have at least 20% more money to work with by saving credit interest.

❖ Indians have a clean fiscal slate because, as a people, they probably have less credit than anyone else. Why develop habits that will impede and limit fiscal acumen?

134

❖ We live in a world of obscene credit card mentality. If you want to raise your income by 20%, quit using credit cards. We have been indoctrinated and programmed to live beyond our means. Once you have been given the stamp of approval and anointed by the establishment, you will have the privilege of spending more money than you make and pay an additional 20% for the privilege! Common sense says that somewhere down the road you will "pay the piper" on the way to fiscal collapse.

❖ Debit cards are a great idea but credit cards are not.

❖ 98% of kids believe that money comes from ATM machines.

❖ Assuming the 10% average growth that the stock market has yielded since 1928, putting away $3,000 a year will build a retirement account of $105,000 after 15 years, $324,000 after 25 years and $894,000 after 35 years.

❖ Get actively involved politically. Register and vote.

❖ Develop a positive physical image that includes confronting alcoholism and obesity. Quit drinking alcohol as a way of life and quit eating frybread as a daily staple.

❖ Nurture unique spirituality.

❖ Maintain cultural affiliation.

The issue of right or wrong is completely obscured by the "spin" of clever lawyers, the media and politics.

Tribal Agenda

❖ Focus on national Indian identity first and tribal affiliation second. Indians are one race of people with 563 tribes, not 563 different races.

❖ Forget archaic tribal animosities and prejudices that often date back hundreds of years. They're ancient history and smack of tribal racism.

❖ Establish progressive and definitive enrollment requirements. These requirements could include several status classifications with commensurate entitlements and responsibilities. Who is and who isn't "Indian" must be redefined

The issue has always been the land and the problem has always been the lack of organization!

by current criteria that will result in a rational and equitable solution. Insidious forces are at work dividing Indians by various categories. The end result is that there are not enough people in any one category to be politically or economically significant.

❖ Aggressively solicit and expand tribal enrollment. Include everyone who meets tribal enrollment qualifications by issuance of a picture enrollment "smart" card. There are at least 15 million people who want to be connected and who are at-large potential Indian votes. Indian traditionalists must realize that in order to survive, they must embrace their urban brethren. It is not prudent for any group to exclude the largest segment (78%) of its constituency.

❖ Reservation Indians and their Urban relatives need each other.

❖ Orchestrate a united tribal voting political coalition on the major Indian issues of health, education and entitlements.

❖ Establish a strategic geographic political agenda. In certain political arenas, a united Indian vote could be the deciding factor in important elections and issues. Every aspect of Indian life is determined by fickle political decisions. Indians live a precarious and fragile political existence.

National Agenda

❖ Develop a strategic campaign to marshal participants and resources. Analyze strengths and weaknesses.

❖ Initiate a national public relations campaign to penetrate the nation's conscience with a sustained multi-faceted professional approach.

❖ Utilize the above public relations campaign to solicit global community opinion and support by exposure of the Indian condition.

❖ Establish specific national concessions as retribution for past grievances.

❖ Establish national political unity to ensure those concessions are mandated.

❖ Develop a national coalition based on economic enterprise networking.

❖ Capitalize on the gaming window of opportunity to establish a basis for long-term social and economic development.

❖ The more successful casinos should contribute a small percentage to tribes with fewer resources and the Urban centers for the general entitlement and education of their relatives.

❖ Get involved with the Internet and the Indian Online portal.

CHAPTER 6 — INDIAN ARMAGEDDON

For the last 100 years, the United States government has initiated compensatory treaty entitlement programs because America took a look in the mirror and didn't like what it saw and had some pangs of conscious. But that brief period of recrimination is over because the nation's conscience has been appeased by the attrition of time and the evolution of more pressing domestic and world crises.

Indian tribes have a "Catch-22" dilemma. They are torn between trying to make the federal government legally live up to its treaty trust responsibilities by funding social and economic programs and at the same time declaring themselves independent sovereign nations.

Indian people need to develop a military campaign mentality because tribal sovereignty and the reservation trust lands are essentially under passive siege. The anti-Indian forces know there is a blood quantum genetic time-bomb ticking and it's just a matter of time.

There are insidious forces at work in Congress today that would love to eliminate the "Indian problem." I believe that in the

The anti-Indian forces know there is a blood quantum genetic time-bomb ticking and it's just a matter of time.

I believe that in the foreseeable future, some bright eyed congressional person will introduce a bill to dissolve the reservation system, divide up the liquidated resources and equitably compensate the entitled Indians.

foreseeable future, some bright eyed congressional person will introduce a bill to dissolve the reservation system, divide up the liquidated resources and equitably compensate the entitled Indians.

Congress cannot use the sword of conquest or beat Indians over the head with the brutal methodology of the past but with the legal thrust of a congressional rapier so smooth that most Indians will hardly know they have been mortally wounded until the damage has been done.

The rationale will go something like this:

❖ "An Indian reservation is an area of land held in trust by the federal government, reserved for Indian use." The Congressional fox is guarding the Indian chicken coop!

❖ The reservation system was an archaic and bad idea in the first place. It's more than 100 years old and Indians are still the poorest race of people in the country with regard to health, education and welfare which is conclusive evidence that the reservation system just doesn't work. Let's take whatever steps are necessary to correct the problem and abolish the system for the well-being of Indian people and the common good of the country.

❖ Only 20% of Indian people live on reservations. The 80% majority have already left the reservations for education and employment opportunities.

❖ The BIA Indian Money Account records are unmanageable and in disarray. The accounting debacle is too old, complex and expensive to resolve.

❖ The reservation allotment records are a fiasco in chaos. The morass of generational fractionation is too old, complex and costly to resolve. The problem continues to grow exponentially with each succeeding generation.

138

❖ The insufficient and limited BIA Budget for Indian programs was:
   ○ $2.3 billion in 2003
   ○ $2.4 billion in 2004
   ○ Requested $2.3 billion in 2005 ($87 million less than the 2004 budget).

❖ The government may need to confiscate the reservation mineral resources for the "common good," but tribes will be justly compensated.

❖ Why should Indians have more special privileges than any other minority citizens? During the development of this country, everyone took their turn in the barrel: the British, Germans, Scottish, Irish, Italians, Africans, Chinese, Japanese, Hispanics, etc. All survived the "pecking order" of integration.

❖ The mandates of "Manifest Destiny" and "Divine Providence" were pre-destined to build and develop the greatest nation in the world. If the Indians still controlled the country and had their way, we would still be hunting buffalo and living in teepees.

❖ After 100 years, many tribal governments are totally dependent on federal support programs with perpetual internal dissention and constant squabbling.

There would be a wailing and gnashing of teeth and a good fight by the 1% Indian minority but the 99% majority would feel relief and enormous benefits of having a final equitable resolution to the long standing "Indian problem." A congressional committee would be formed to deal with the problem and, if the Indians were lucky, the fight might even go right down party lines!

If the Indians are counting on what is right, fair, just and legal, think again about the long history between the Indian people and the United States government. Nobody ever said life was going to be fair!

There are also anti-Indian forces in Congress that advocate the dissolution of the reservation system as a means to confiscate reservation resources for the "good of the country."

Congress at Work

The Clinton impeachment hearings were a disturbing insight into the Congressional political process. At first blush, the issues were clear and a course of action seemed appropriate and inevitable. An immoral president got caught with his pants down in the Oval Office with a 22-year-old employee and then lied about a number of issues, under oath, to the American public. (We've heard the details ad nauseum.) His conduct was totally unacceptable and was condemned by everyone, especially the politicians. Republicans and Democrats alike were publicly outraged and demanded immediate resignation for the good of the country.

Fast forward six months. The issue of right or wrong is completely obscured by the "spin" of clever lawyers, the media and politics. The bottom line is that the decision of whether or not to remove a president from office was decided by a political committee divided almost exactly down party lines. This democratic decision supposedly reflected the "will" of the people and what was good for the country.

Anti-Indian Forces at Work

There are some 50 anti-Indian organizations with patriotic sounding names and acronyms that are busy and working hard to usurp Indian entitlements and lands. Five coordinating organizations and two national organizations have been created by the anti-Indian movement mainly in the states of Washington, Montana, Minnesota, and Wisconsin (not including organizations with other agendas which closely identify with the movement) by 1991.

Though the anti-Indian movement is held together with a lot of smoke and mirrors, there is enough substance to it to seriously threaten the peace and stability of Indian tribes in the United States.

There are also anti-Indian forces in Congress that advocate the dissolution of the reservation system as a means to confiscate reservation resources for the "good of the country."

Window of Opportunity

Less than 15% of the 563 tribes are successful enough to make per capita payments to tribal members. That per capita ranges from stipends to sizeable monthly payments. The majority of the tribal gaming operations are marginal and most tribes have a huge void of basic necessities such as housing, health care, schools, roads, etc. A handful of tribes (for example, Mashantucket Pequot's Foxwoods Casino, Shakopee Sioux's Mystic Lake Casino) are enjoying enormous success. They are tribes that generate almost all of the Indian gaming publicity.

The more successful gaming tribes should form an economic alliance organization to help build Indian businesses. They should also build an American Indian University that is second to none in all disciplines such as medicine, law, science, etc. The Howard University for African Americans is a good model.

For those tribes with relatively small membership and proximity to large customer base, the casinos seem to be a quick-fix basis for cash flow. A short term solution for long-term problems.

What will be the attitude of the federal government and the public towards subsidy programs as the tribal coffers fill?

For the first time in history, Indian tribes have some resources and a window of opportunity to build a power base that could secure the future of all Indian people for generations to come. When one Indian tribe loses, all tribes lose.

For the first time in history, Indian tribes have some resources and a window of opportunity to build a power base that could secure the future of all Indian people for generations to come.

Survival One More Time

Several factors make American Indian tribes a unique minority in this country:

- ❖ They are the indigenous natives of this country.
- ❖ They have inherent tribal sovereignty.
- ❖ They have a trust land base.

Tribal affiliation doesn't have to be either/or; there can be degrees of recognition and benefits based on blood quantum or some other form of inequality.

If American Indians could ever come together under a common banner and capitalize on their unique advantages, their collective voice would echo down the halls of Congress.

Let's revisit the Indian demographic scenario once more:

❖ 22% of the Indian population live on reservation.
❖ 78% of the Indian population live off reservation.
❖ Three out of 4 Indians do not marry other Indians.

Do the math and theoretically, in about two more generations, the vast majority of Indians who live off reservation will no longer be considered Indians because of the blood quantum quagmire.

An educated guess would be that 98% of the Indian population are already tribally hyphenated within geographic regions (Chippewa-Cherokee-Sioux-Potawatomi, etc.) and the majority are racially hyphenated (Chippewa-Cherokee-Irish-English-African, etc.).

Keeping verifiable records of the infinite number of tribal and racial admixture combinations would be like trying to solve a huge blood quantum Rubik's Cube.

If Indians can come to terms with the blood quantum issue, and get organized they will survive and could become stronger economically and politically. If they do not, they will probably not survive as we know Indians today.

Indians who live on the reservations will survive the blood quantum screening for several generations longer, but will eventually meet the same end.

Indians must find a way to engage the support of that vast reservoir of people who claim Indian ancestry and those who are empathizers to a common cause, and still leave room for some avarice.

Tribal affiliation doesn't have to be either/or; there can be degrees of recognition and benefits based on blood quantum or some other form of inequality. Most people outside the inner circle of enrolled tribal members simply want the recognition and acknowledgement of their birthright.

The Indian people who live off-reservation and the Indian people who live on reservation need each other. The two camps should complement each other, rather than be considered adversaries. Each component brings unique talents to the table and each has a mission in the big scheme of things.

I see no inconsistency between Urban Indian with their education, street smarts and business acumen working in concert with their Reservation counterparts who retain precious spiritual, language, ceremonial and traditional connectivity. The reservations should be a welcome refuge where the exiled can rejuvenate their family and tribal connectivity.

American Indians have the talent, some political money and enough voters in certain parts of the country to impose their agenda on the political process and take control of their destiny.

What other race of people have the unprecedented opportunity to influence the course of their destiny that American Indians have? Will American Indians rise to the occasion and seize the opportunity to unite or will they self-destruct by the self-imposed blood quantum malaise and internal political cannibalism?

American Indians have the responsibility, to those ancestors who fired arrows against cannons and survived against overwhelming odds, to make that survival meaningful.

> *American Indians have the responsibility, to those ancestors who fired arrows against cannons and survived against overwhelming odds, to make that survival meaningful.*

Notes:

_____

_____

_____

_____

_____

_____

_____

_____

_____

_____

_____

_____

_____

Section 4:
Genealogy

Scientists at Howard University are working on Mitochondrial DNA studies which indicate that there are millions of Americans who probably have an Indian ancestor.

Color of Racism

As man adapted to his geographic environment, he developed certain physical characteristics, learned to walk upright, lost some body hair, and became a social creature. Tribalism became a basic instinct, based on fear, which was essential for survival. Racism is a mutation of tribalism that evolved from fear to hate. Tribalism to the extreme mutates into racism. Racism is learned and generational. Most people still have some degree of tribalism for the simple reason that they are most comfortable around people like themselves.

Racism is socially archaic, maliciously ignorant, and nonproductive. It becomes an insidious emotional cancer that leaves the carrier mentally stunted. Mental evolution has simply not kept pace with social evolution. In today's society, human similarities are more important than racial differences.

Within the next couple of generations, racism as we know it will be a moot issue, a done deal. The racial train has left the station. Even hard-core racists need only look at their grandchildren. Racism is a waste of time on a foregone conclusion. Each race must come to terms with its vested interest in other races and lay the issue to rest.

The ideals of democracy are a tribute to man's conceptual humanity. Only human nature stands in the way. It is neither rational nor moral for those who enjoy the tenets of democracy to deny those same basic rights to others because of their difference in appearance or ideology.

In *The Emperor's New Clothes* by Joseph L. Graves, Jr., a professor of Evolutionary Biology at Arizona State University, there's a great deal of in-depth research to support the author's premise that there is no scientific basis for the theory of biological races. There is only biological diversity within the biological human race.

An American paradox: On one hand, racial diversity is one source of the nation's strength and yet on the other, it's the source of some of its worst social problems. Like it or not, racial diversity is an inherent component of American society, and America is an inherent component of a global community.

Through DNA genetic testing, we are discovering that historically, racial blood mixing was more prevalent and widespread than anyone realized. When the "nature of the beast" is factored in the equation, who can say with absolute certainty that they know the race of every ancestor for 500 years?

For years, Howard University has used genetic data to study diseases that afflict African-Americans. A side benefit is that genetic testing can be used to help African-Americans discover their ancestral origins in Africa and in America.

African-Americans, who descended from people brought to America as slaves 350 years ago, are not so African anymore. The tests have revealed that most African-Americans, no matter how dark their complexion, can claim at least one white or American Indian ancestor.

The "Brotherhood of Man"

Whenever a majority has dominance and control over a smaller "inferior" ethnic group, the "nature of the beast" takes its liberties by the unwritten code, "to the victor belongs the spoils." Genetic admixture was a prevalent and common practice between the Euro-Americans and the two ethnic groups at the bottom of the American socioeconomic spectrum, the African slaves and the Indians.

The genetic admixture with slaves commenced, from the beginning, on the slave ships. The slave owners, their relatives and the overseers continued the practice and considered it a rite of passage. The practice was not publicly acknowledged for generations and if the progeny were acknowledged at all, it was with a "wink" as the "skeleton in the family closet."

Recent acknowledgements, however grudgingly, have given the "brotherhood of man" a much deeper meaning and significance than has been acknowledged in the past.

We now know conclusively through DNA evidence that Thomas Jefferson had a long-term relationship with his slave Sally Hemings and probably fathered one or more of her children. This relationship was portrayed as consensual but it has always been common knowledge that female slaves were often rape victims or mistresses of white plantation owners or overseers. The genetic pyramid created by bi-racial pairing over the generations is enormous. Thomas Jefferson, George Washington and now Strom Thurmond have been "outed." If these public figures and members of the aristocracy were culpable, one would feel safe in saying that the lower echelons of society were certainly active to a much greater degree.

Genetic admixture self-generates exponentially with each succeeding generation into pyramid form. The width of the pyramid base is expedited by large families. When a DNA analysis becomes cost effective and common, there are going to be a awful lot of surprised people!

Several years ago, one study indicated that as a result of genetic admixture during slavery, there are some 28 million people who have a discernible degree of African blood and aren't aware of it.

This is in addition to the people on both sides of the color line during slavery who acknowledged progeny such as the Mulattoes, the Quadroons and the Octoroons. The "One Drop" doctrine, whereby one "drop" of black blood made one black was a social and legal convention originated to keep the progeny of master-slave liaisons as slaves.

America must resolve the issues of domestic racism before undertaking the problems of a multi-cultural global market. There are six billion people on this tiny planet and America's 280 million people are only 5% of the world market. America cannot afford racism.

If human development is viewed from a telescopic galaxy perspective, racism becomes insignificant. The further removed from the situation, the less important it becomes. Americans have more pressing matters to deal with than the blood composition or the skin pigmentation of their neighbors.

Indians come in all colors, from blue-eyed blondes to buffalo soldiers. The racial lines have blurred over the generations. The blending is accelerated by mobility and changes in social attitudes.

The beauty and abundance of multi-racial people on television, in the movies and on university campuses neutralizes much of the bigotry.

Indians need to be conscious and wary of practicing insidious racism. Dissension and prejudice permeate nearly every aspect of Indian life. It is ironic that some Indians practice a kind of racism they endured for hundreds of years. A racism that nearly exterminated the Indian people. Tribal racism has kept the Indian tribes divided, vulnerable and manageable.

Do You Have an Indian Ancestor?

We get more inquiries related to genealogy than anything else. The inquiries usually go like this: "How do I go about establishing my Indian genealogy and become a tribal member? I know that I had a great-great-great Indian ancestor, I believe she was a Cherokee Princess, but older family members were vague or refused to talk about it."

American Indians have been mixing inter-tribally for at least 12,000 years and interracially for 500 years, the chances are pretty good that untold millions of Americans probably have an American Indian ancestor.

Howard University researchers are using genetic testing methods to link millions of African-Americans to the part of Africa their ancestors hailed from. They have gotten positive results from African-Americans already tested and hope to market such a service by this summer. Marketing details will be worked out and the tests will be offered to the public in the price range of $200 to $300.

African-Americans descended from people brought here over a period of more than 350 years are not so African anymore. Tests have already revealed that about 30 percent of African males have a white male ancestor often evidence one of their slave ancestors was the rape victim or mistress of a white plantation owner or overseer. Most African-Americans, no matter how dark their complexion, can claim at least one white or Indian ancestor, geneticists said.

The point is that because Indians have been mixing inter-tribally for thousands of years and interracially for 500 years, the chances are pretty good that untold millions of Americans probably have an Indian ancestor.

How Can I Become Tribally Enrolled?

Tribal enrollment criteria are set forth in tribal constitutions, articles of incorporation or ordinances. The criterion varies from tribe to tribe, so uniform membership requirements do not exist.

Two common requirements for membership are lineal descendants from someone named on the tribe's base roll or relationship to a tribal member who descended from someone named on the base roll. (A "base roll" is the original list of members as designated in a tribal constitution or other document specifying enrollment criteria.) Other conditions such as tribal blood quantum, tribal residency, or continued contact with the tribe are common.

After you have completed your genealogical research, documented your ancestry, and determined the tribe with which your ancestor was affiliated, you are ready to contact the tribe directly to obtain the criteria for membership. Each tribe determines whether an individual is eligible for membership. Each tribe maintains it's own enrollment records and records about past members.

What are the Benefits and Services of Enrollment?

There has long been a myth that Indians receive a monthly check from the United States government because of their status as Indians. There is no basis for this belief. Some tribes, tribal members and lineal descendants received payments from the federal government resulting from claims settlements. Very few judgment funds per capita payments remain today.

Some tribes distribute payments to enrolled members when revenues from the sale of tribal assets such as timber, hydroelectric power or oil and gas permit. Many tribes cannot make per capita payments because they do not have natural resources or other revenue from which they make a fund distribution.

There is a clear distinction between judgment funds and tribal funds. Judgment funds are appropriated by congress after a claim that is filed by tribes or Indian descendant groups against the United States is settled. Tribal funds are derived from tribal assets (refer to paragraph above). An individual does not have to be an enrolled member of a tribe to receive a final judgment fund payment. An individual must be an enrolled member of a tribe to be eligible to receive payments derived from tribal funds.

The BIA, through its government-to-government relationship with federally recognized tribes, carries out the federal government's unique and continuing relationship with and responsibility to tribes and Indian people. BIA programs support and assist federally-recognized tribes in the development of tribal governments, strong economies and quality programs. The scope of BIA programs is extensive and includes a range of services comparable to the programs of state and local government, e.g., education, social services, law enforcement, courts, real estate services, agriculture and range management and resource protection.

Many federal agencies other than the BIA have special programs to serve the American Indian population, i.e., the Indian Health Service (IHS), an adjunct of the Public Health Service, Department of Health and Human Services (DHHS). The IHS provides health care services through a network of reservation-based hospitals and clinics. Besides standard medical care, the agency has established programs that specialize in maternal and child health, mental health, substance abuse, home health care, nutrition, etc.

The Administration for Indians, another agency within DHHS, administers programs aimed at strengthening tribal governments and supporting the social and economic development of reservation communities. Other agencies of the federal government that serves the special needs of Indian people include the departments of Housing and Urban Development, Justice, Agriculture, Education, Labor, Commerce and Energy.

All Indians, whether they live on or off reservations, are eligible (like all other citizens who meet eligibility requirements) to receive services provided by the state such as Temporary Assistance for Needy Families (TANF), Supplemental Security Income (SSI), the Food Stamp Program and the Low Income Heating and Energy Assistance Program (LIHEAP).

Contacting a Tribal Entity

The Bureau of Indian Affairs publishes a list of federally recognized Indian tribes in the *Federal Register*. The latest publication was on December 30, 1998, which can be obtained from most libraries or accessed on the Internet. (See Internet address listings in the Bibliography.)

How Do I Begin My Genealogy Research?

The research of your "family tree" as a document for future generations is up to you.

The federal government does not do family research, nor does its National Archives collect or preserve family trees. Books on family history and genealogy are collected, complied and published by private individuals who do so because they are interested descendants.

As the depository of the federal government's records deemed of permanent value for historical purposes, the National Archives houses many records that can be helpful to persons who wish to trace their ancestry. The search, however, cannot be completed at the National Archives alone. Many other depositories should be consulted. Following are suggestions about things to do and ways to go about getting a start at finding your ancestors:

The Internet

Our best advice is to explore and experiment with the tremendous explosion of genealogy resources on the Internet. A good place to start is Cyndi's List. (See Bibliography for web address.)

Computer Programs

There are a number of genealogy computer programs at your local computer store that will provide you with structure and format.

Start With Yourself

You are the trunk of your family tree and it branches out from you. Start with yourself, the known, and work toward the unknown. You should find out all the vital information you can about your parents, write it down, then find out about your grandparents, great-grandparents, etc.

Names, Dates, Places, Relationships

You will be concerned with pulling from the many and varied documents of recorded history's four key items names, places, dates and relationships. These are the tools of the family researcher. People can be identified in records by their names, the dates of events in their lives (birth, marriage, death), the places they lived and the relationships to others either stated or implied in the records.

Home Sources

The first place to begin is at home. You can find much information in family bibles, newspaper clippings, military certificates, birth and death certificates, marriage licenses, diaries, letters, scrapbooks, backs of pictures, baby books, etc.

Relatives as Source

Visit or write those in your family who may have information, particularly older relatives. More often than not, others before you have gathered data about the families in which you are interested. You should write a letter, make a personal visit, or conduct a telephone survey to find out about such persons and what information is already collected.

Finding Distant Relatives

Before launching your research program in libraries and archives, search for distant relatives who may have already performed research. Advertise in the local genealogical bulletins (city, county or state) where your ancestors lived.

Birth, Marriage and Death Records

Most states have a Department of Vital Records that keeps records of birth, deaths, marriages and divorces. Birth and death registration became a requirement around the turn of the century, about 1890–1915. Before that time these events will be found recorded generally in church records and family bibles. Marriages will be found recorded in most counties, dating often as early as the establishment of the county.

Church Records

Each Mormon Church or The Church of Jesus Christ of Latter Day Saints has a Family History Center, usually staffed by volunteers, that is linked to the national archives in Salt Lake City. Mormons are one of the best and most competent genealogy resources available and they have a particular interest in Indian genealogy.

A few churches have records of important events in the lives of members but many do not. Investigate the possibility of finding genealogical data in the records of the church to which your ancestor belonged.

Deeds and Wills

Records of property acquisition and disposition can be good sources of genealogical data. Such records are normally in the county courthouses. Often the earliest county records or copies of them are also available in state archives.

Federal Records

The National Archives in Washington, DC, has records of use in genealogical research. The federal census made every 10 years since 1790 is a good source. The census records are also available on microfilm in the National Archives' regional branches located in 11 metropolitan areas throughout the country (description leaflet available upon request). The National Archives also has military service and related records, passenger arrival records and others. (See Bibliography for contact information.)

Libraries, Societies, Archives

Visit the state, regional and local institutions in your area. Libraries, historical and genealogical societies and archival depositories are all good sources for genealogical and family history data.

Genealogy is Fun, Exciting and Rewarding

The detective work and research of genealogy is an exciting and rewarding activity. Each person is entitled to acknowledgement of their ancestry.

Section 5:
Study Guide

American Indian anthropology in this country is a vast, complex and diverse subject. It would take a lifetime of study to understand Indians' true place in history. The goal of the *American Indian Facts of Life* Handbook and this Study Guide is to present enough information, direction and reference to motivate you to do further study and research in your area of interest.

When you can answer most of the 38 questions in this Study Guide, you will know more about today's American Indians than 99.9% of the general public, including Indians.

This Study Guide format is fill-in blanks with essay questions that may be answered on a separate sheet of paper. All answers to all questions are found in the *"American Indian Facts of Life."*

This Study Guide can be downloaded and multiple copies printed for classroom use at: *www.nativedata.com/studyguide.*

Population

The United States government's definition of a legal Indian :

Any person who has the certifiable Indian blood quantum to meet the enrollment requirements of a federally-recognized tribe.

1. Census 2000 enumerates the Indian population at
   _____ million.

2. Of that population, approximately _____ million are tribally enrolled.

3. There are approximately _____ million people in the United States who have a discernible degree of Indian blood.

4. The total Indian population is less than _____ % of the total United States population.

5. Approximately _____ % of the Indian population live on reservations.

6. Approximately _____ % of the Indian population are Urban Indians.

7. Do you think the Urban Indian population will increase or decrease by 2050? (Explain your answer on a separate sheet of paper.)

8. Do you think the Reservation Indian population will increase or decrease by 2050? (Explain your answer on a separate sheet of paper.)

9. Do you think the enrolled Indian population will increase or decrease by 2050? (Explain your answer on a separate sheet of paper.)

Tribes

The United States government's definition for a federally-recognized tribe:

Any Indian tribe, band, nation, rancheria, pueblo, colony or community which is recognized by the United States government as eligible for the special programs and services provided by the Secretary of the Interior to Indians because of their status as Indians.

1. There are _____ federally-recognized tribes in the United States.

2. There are approximately _____ state-recognized tribes.

3. Approximately _____ tribes are petitioning for federal recognition.

4. Each tribe has the right to determine the requirements for tribal _____ .

159

5. Certifiable _____ _____ is a basic requirement for tribal enrollment.

6. The _____ Nation of Oklahoma has the most enrolled members.

7. Approximately _____ % of Indians live on reservations.

8. Approximately _____ % of Indians live off reservation.

9. In your opinion, what is the future of Indian tribes as blood quantum is diluted through the natural process of inter-tribal and inter-racial assimilation? (Explain your answer on a separate sheet of paper.)

10. How could these tribes network politically and economically to achieve common goals? (Explain your answer on a separate sheet of paper.)

Reservations

A federally-recognized Indian reservation is:

An area of land held in trust by the federal government reserved for Indian use.

1. There are _____ federally-recognized reservations in the United States.

2. These federally-recognized reservations are considered _____ nations.

3. These reservations occupy approximately _____ million acres.

4. Approximately _____ % are reservation trust lands.

5. Approximately _____ % are allotted lands.

6. The Department of _____ is the trustee of the United States government.

7. The Bureau of _____ _____ is responsible for the administration and management of the trust responsibilities.

8. The state of _____ has the greatest number of reservations.

9. The state of _____ has the largest reservation.

10. Approximately _____ % of the Indians live on reservations.

11. What is your understanding of Indian reservations as sovereign nations? (Explain your answer on a separate sheet of paper.)

Just The Facts

1. Indians were categorically granted United States citizenship in (year) _____ .

2. Indians granted the right to vote in Arizona in (year) _____ .

3. Indians granted the right to vote in New Mexico in (year) _____ .

4. The United States is divided into a total of _____ BIA Regional Offices.

5. From 1778 to 1871, there were _____ treaties negotiated with Indian tribes.

161

6. Approximately _____ tribes were relocated to Oklahoma Indian Territory during the 1800s.

7. The government spends $ _____ billion annually on Indian programs.

8. In your opinion, have Indians been socially and/or economically disadvantaged? (Explain your answer on a separate sheet of paper.)

Notes:

_____

_____

_____

_____

_____

_____

_____

_____

_____

_____

_____

_____

_____

Notes:

_____

_____

_____

_____

_____

_____

_____

_____

_____

_____

_____

Section 6:
Bibliography

The Internet has dramatically changed the way people do research. Most of the reports and lists used in the original edition of this book are no longer available in print. Most of the revisions and updated information for this printing are compiled from Internet websites.

Whenever possible, our website: *www.nativedata.com* is linked to sites than enhance or contain information that is relative.

2004 Tribal Leaders List

The 2004 Tribal Leaders list contains contact information for all (12) Bureau of Indian Affairs Regional Offices and all Tribal Leaders. Visit *www.doi.gov/leaders.pdf*

Internet Resource Links

The Bureau of Indian Affairs website offers extensive linking to Indian resource websites. Visit *www.doi.gov/bureau-Indian-affairs.html* for links to most Indian organization websites.

Data Resources

Native Data Network (*www.nativedata.com*)

Tribal Data Resources (*www.tdronline.com*)

Indian Business Organizations

Indian Business Association
(*www.Indian-american-bus.org*)

National Center for American Indian
Enterprise Development (*www.ncaied.org*)

Indian Publications

Native Peoples Magazine (*www.nativepeoples.com*)

Indian Country Today (*www.Indiancountry.com*)

News From Indian Country (*www.indiancountrynews.com*)

Catalogs of Indian Publications

American Indian Science & Engineering Society
(*www.aises.org*)

Four Winds Trading Company
(*www.fourwinds-trading.com*)

Four Winds Indian Books (*www.fourwindsbooks.com*)

Indian Public Broadcasting Consortium
(*www.Indiantelecom.org*)

Smithsonian Institution Press
(*www.si.edu/organiza/offices/sipress*)

The Falmouth Institute (*www.falmouthinst.com*)

States That Do NOT Have Indian Affairs Offices

To my knowledge, the governors and legislatures in the following states have not created official Indian affairs offices, commissions, or councils:

1. Alaska
2. Arkansas
3. Delaware
4. Georgia
5. Idaho
6. Illinois
7. Kansas
8. Kentucky
9. Louisiana
10. Mississippi
11. Missouri
12. New Hampshire
13. New York
14. Ohio
15. Pennsylvania
16. Rhode Island
17. South Carolina
18. Texas
19. Vermont
20. West Virginia
21. Wisconsin